WILLIAMS-SONOMA

FOODMADEFAST

# salad

RECIPES
Brigit L. Binns

GENERAL EDITOR
Chuck Williams

PHOTOGRAPHY
Tucker + Hossler

# contents

**20 MINUTES START TO FINISH**

# about this book

Today, as busy cooks seek fresh flavors and fast, healthful options, salads have come front and center as meals in their own right. This book shows you how easy it can be to create satisfying main-dish salads in a matter of minutes. The recipes make the most of a handful of well-chosen ingredients for outstanding flavor with minimal effort. Most can be on the table in less than half an hour. Others require just fifteen minutes of hands-on prep, freeing up your time for other tasks.

You'll find everything from innovative versions of classics such as Grilled Chicken Caesar and Niçoise Salad with Salmon to bold international favorites like Vietnamese Shrimp & Noodle Salad and Mediterranean Meze. These bountiful dinner salads offer proof that great food made fast is a simple matter of organization, smart shopping, and, most of all, easy, foolproof recipes. Add bread, and you and your family can sit down to a stress-free, home-cooked meal any night of the week.

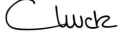

20 minutes
start to finish

# chicken & orzo
## salad

**Pesto,** ⅔ cup (5 fl oz/160 ml)

**White wine vinegar,**
2 tablespoons

**Salt and freshly ground
pepper**

**Olive oil,** 3 tablespoons

**Orzo pasta,** ¾ lb (375 g)

**Cooked chicken, poached
(page 26) or rotisserie,**
2½ cups (1 lb/500 g)
shredded

**Cherry tomatoes,** ½ lb
(250 g), halved

**Baby spinach,** 6 oz (185 g)

SERVES 4

### 1 Make the vinaigrette
In a large bowl, whisk together the pesto, vinegar,
¼ teaspoon salt, and a pinch of pepper. Gradually whisk in the
oil until smooth.

### 2 Cook the orzo
Bring a large pot of water to a boil. Add 2 tablespoons
salt and the orzo. Cook, stirring occasionally to prevent sticking,
until the pasta is al dente, according to the package directions.
Drain, rinse under cold running water, and drain again. Add the
orzo to the vinaigrette and toss to coat evenly.

### 3 Assemble the salad
Add the chicken, tomatoes, and spinach to the orzo and
toss gently to combine, then serve.

## cook's tip

In the past, if you wanted to
serve pesto, you had to make it
from scratch. Now it is available
in plastic containers in the
refrigerated section of many
markets. Avoid the pesto sold
in glass jars on store shelves,
as the fresh basil flavor is lost.

## cook's tip

Unlike many fruits, pears ripen off
the tree, and they ripen from the
inside out, so they may feel very
firm on the surface even when
soft inside. To test for ripeness,
press just to one side of the stem
end; if it gives, the pear is ripe.
To ripen pears quickly, put them
in a paper bag along with a
banana. Check once a day to see
how the ripening is progressing.

# spinach, pear & walnut salad

## 1 Toast the walnuts

Preheat the oven to 350°F (180°C). Spread the walnuts on a baking sheet and toast, stirring occasionally, until aromatic, 8–10 minutes; do not let them brown.

## 2 Make the dressing

Meanwhile, in a large bowl, whisk together the sour cream, mayonnaise, walnut oil, vinegar, Worcestershire sauce, hot-pepper sauce, and a pinch of pepper until smooth.

## 3 Assemble the salad

Add the spinach, pears, and walnuts to the dressing and toss to coat evenly. Arrange on plates or in bowls, sprinkle with the cheese, and serve.

**Walnut halves,** ¾ cup (3 oz/90 g)

**Sour cream,** ¼ cup (2 oz/ 60 g)

**Mayonnaise,** 2 tablespoons

**Walnut oil,** 2 tablespoons

**Red wine vinegar,** 2 teaspoons

**Worcestershire sauce,** 1 teaspoon

**Hot-pepper sauce,** dash

**Freshly ground pepper**

**Baby spinach,** 6 oz (185 g)

**Pears such as Bosc or Anjou,** 4, peeled, halved, cored, and cut into thin wedges

**Blue cheese,** 2 oz (60 g), crumbled

SERVES 4

# turkey cobb salad

**White wine vinegar,**
2 tablespoons

**Dijon mustard,** 2 teaspoons

**Worcestershire sauce,**
1 teaspoon

**Mayonnaise,** ¼ cup
(2 fl oz/60 ml)

**Olive oil,** ¼ cup (2 fl oz/
60 ml)

**Salt and freshly ground
pepper**

**Blue cheese,** ¼ lb (125 g),
crumbled

**Thick-cut bacon,** 8 slices,
chopped

**Iceberg lettuce,** 1 head,
cored and thinly sliced

**Avocados,** 2 small, peeled,
pitted, and cubed

**Plum (Roma) tomatoes,**
4 small, chopped

**Smoked turkey breast,**
½ lb (250 g), cubed

SERVES 4

1 **Make the dressing**
In a large bowl, whisk together the vinegar, mustard, Worcestershire sauce, mayonnaise, oil, and a pinch of pepper until smooth. Stir in one-fourth of the cheese.

2 **Fry the bacon**
In a heavy frying pan over medium-low heat, cook the bacon, stirring occasionally, until crisp, about 5 minutes. Using a slotted spoon, transfer to paper towels to drain.

3 **Assemble the salad**
Add the lettuce to the dressing and toss to coat evenly. Taste and adjust the seasoning with salt and pepper. Divide the lettuce among plates and arrange the avocados, tomatoes, and turkey on top. Sprinkle with the bacon and the remaining cheese, and serve.

## cook's tip

To make candied pecans for sprinkling in the salad, line a baking sheet with parchment (baking) paper. In a saucepan over medium heat, bring ½ cup (4 oz/125 g) sugar and ¼ cup (2 fl oz/60 ml) water to a boil and cook until light amber. Add 1 cup (4 oz/125 g) pecan halves, swirl the pan, then pour onto the prepared sheet and spread the nuts in a single layer. Let cool.

# grapefruit, jicama
# & avocado salad

### 1 Prepare the grapefruit

Trim a slice from the top and bottom of the grapefruit, cutting through the peel and pith. Stand the grapefruit upright, and following the contour of the fruit, cut away the peel and pith, being careful not to remove too much of the flesh. Holding the grapefruit over a large bowl to catch the juice, cut between the membranes to release each segment. Cut the segments into pieces and set aside in a separate bowl. Repeat with the remaining grapefruit.

### 2 Make the vinaigrette

Add the vinegar, mustard, ¼ teaspoon salt, and a pinch of pepper to the grapefruit juice and whisk to combine. Gradually whisk in the oil until smooth. Stir in the basil.

### 3 Assemble the salad

Add the radicchio, jicama, and grapefruit pieces to the vinaigrette and toss to coat evenly. Arrange on plates, top with the avocado, and serve.

**Ruby grapefruits,** 2

**White wine vinegar,** 1 tablespoon

**Honey Dijon mustard,** 1 teaspoon

**Salt and freshly ground pepper**

**Olive oil,** ⅓ cup (3 fl oz/ 80 ml)

**Fresh basil,** 1 tablespoon minced

**Radicchio,** 1 small head, cored and thinly sliced

**Jicama,** about ½ lb (250 g), peeled and cut into matchsticks

**Avocados,** 2, peeled, pitted, and cut into chunks

**SERVES 4**

# thai steak &
# bok choy salad

**Skirt steak,** 1 ¼ lb (625 g),
at room temperature

**Canola oil,** ¼ cup (2 fl oz/
60 ml), plus 2 tablespoons

**Salt and freshly ground
pepper**

**Lime juice,** from 2 limes

**Garlic,** 2 cloves, minced

**Shallot,** 1, minced

**Hot or spicy mustard,**
1 teaspoon

**Soy sauce,** 1 tablespoon

**Asian fish sauce,**
2 tablespoons

**Mixed baby greens,** 5 oz
(155 g)

**Fresh mint leaves,** ¼ cup
(¼ oz/7 g)

**Baby bok choy,** 2 heads,
bases, tops, and tough leaves
trimmed and thinly sliced
crosswise

SERVES 4

1 **Season the steak and make the dressing**
Prepare a gas or charcoal grill for direct grilling over
high heat. Alternatively, preheat a grill pan over high heat.
Brush both sides of the steak with the 2 tablespoons oil and
season generously with salt and pepper. In a large bowl,
whisk together the lime juice, garlic, shallot, mustard, soy sauce,
fish sauce, and ¼ teaspoon pepper. Gradually whisk in the
¼ cup oil until smooth.

2 **Grill the steak**
Place the steak on the grill rack or in the grill pan and
cook, turning once, 2–4 minutes per side for rare or medium-
rare. Transfer to a cutting board and let stand for 5–10 minutes.

3 **Assemble the salad**
Add the greens, mint, and bok choy to the dressing
and toss to coat evenly. Arrange on plates. Cut the steak on the
diagonal across the grain into thin slices. Place the slices on
the greens and serve.

## cook's tip

Nearly any steak, cooked
rare or medium-rare, can b
substituted for the skirt
steak. Flank and sirloin
are both good options.

This recipe is also a great
way to use leftover steak.
Bring 1 lb (500 g) of cooke
steak to room temperature
for about 15 minutes
before slicing and adding
to the salad.

## cook's tip

The toasted bread crumbs can
be sprinkled on vegetables, pasta,
pizza, and egg dishes such as
a frittata, as well as other salads,
to add crisp texture and garlicky
flavor. Store the crumbs in
an airtight container at room
temperature for 3 days or
in the freezer for a few months.

# tuna & white bean salad

1 **Toast the bread crumbs**
In a frying pan over medium heat, warm the 1 tablespoon oil. Add the bread crumbs and a pinch each of salt and pepper. Cook, stirring occasionally, just until the crumbs begin to brown, about 5 minutes. Add the garlic, remove from the heat, and stir for 1 minute longer.

2 **Make the vinaigrette**
In a large serving bowl, whisk together the lemon juice, mustard, ¼ teaspoon salt, and a pinch of pepper. Gradually whisk in the ⅓ cup oil until smooth.

3 **Assemble the salad**
Add the parsley, beans, celery, onion, and tuna to the vinaigrette and toss gently to coat evenly. Arrange the lettuce on plates and top with the tuna and bean mixture. Sprinkle with the toasted bread crumbs and serve.

**Olive oil,** ⅓ cup (3 fl oz/ 80 ml), plus 1 tablespoon

**Fresh bread crumbs,** ⅔ cup (1 ½ oz/45 g)

**Salt and freshly ground pepper**

**Garlic,** 1 clove, minced

**Lemon juice,** from 1 lemon

**Whole-grain mustard,** 2 teaspoons

**Flat-leaf (Italian) parsley,** ¼ cup (⅓ oz/10 g) coarsely chopped

**White beans,** 1 can (15 oz/470 g), rinsed and drained

**Celery,** 2 stalks, chopped

**Red onion,** ½ small, halved lengthwise and cut into slivers

**Tuna packed in olive oil,** 2 cans (6 oz/185 g each), drained and flaked

**Butter (Boston) lettuce,** 2 heads, pale inner leaves only

SERVES 4

# spanish
# chicken salad

**Olive oil,** ¼ cup (2 fl oz/ 60 ml), plus 2 teaspoons

**Slivered almonds,** ¾ cup (3 oz/90 g)

**Garlic,** 2 cloves, minced

**Paprika, preferably Spanish smoked,** 1 teaspoon

**Sherry vinegar,** 2 tablespoons

**Mayonnaise,** 2 tablespoons

**Salt and freshly ground pepper**

**Green- or red-leaf lettuce,** 1 head, torn into bite-sized pieces

**Cooked chicken, poached (page 26) or rotisserie,** 4 cups (1½ lb/750 g) shredded

**Jarred roasted red bell peppers (capsicums),** 2, sliced

SERVES 4

1 Toast the almonds
In a small frying pan over medium heat, warm the 2 teaspoons oil. Add the almonds and toast, stirring, until crisp and golden, 5–7 minutes. Transfer to a plate.

2 Make the vinaigrette
In a large bowl, whisk together the garlic, paprika, vinegar, mayonnaise, ½ teaspoon salt, and a pinch of pepper. Gradually whisk in the ¼ cup oil until smooth.

3 Assemble the salad
Add the lettuce, chicken, almonds, and bell peppers to the vinaigrette and toss to coat evenly. Arrange on individual plates and serve.

## cook's tip

For picnic pita sandwiches, make the salad as directed, but pit and chop the olives. Slice leftover grilled, poached (page 26), or purchased rotisserie chicken breasts and toss with the salad. Halve the pita rounds, stuff with the salad and chicken, and serve.

# greek salad
# with herbed pita

### 1 Make the vinaigrette

In a large bowl, whisk together the lemon juice, garlic, and a generous amount of pepper. Gradually whisk in the ¼ cup oil until smooth.

### 2 Warm the pita

Preheat the oven to 300°F (150°C). Cut each pita into 4 wedges. Arrange on a baking sheet and brush both sides with the 2 tablespoons oil. Sprinkle with the oregano and place in the oven to warm for about 10 minutes.

### 3 Assemble the salad

Meanwhile, add the lettuce, cucumber, and tomatoes to the vinaigrette and toss to coat evenly. Arrange on plates and top with the olives, feta, and green onions. Place the warm pita wedges alongside the salads and serve.

**Lemon juice,** from 1 lemon

**Garlic,** 1 clove, minced

**Freshly ground pepper**

**Olive oil,** ¼ cup (2 fl oz/ 60 ml), plus 2 tablespoons

**Pita bread,** 4 rounds

**Dried oregano,** ½ teaspoon

**Hearts of romaine (cos) lettuce,** 2, coarsely chopped

**English (hothouse) cucumber,** halved crosswise and thickly sliced

**Tomatoes,** 2, cut into wedges

**Assorted brine-cured olives,** 1 cup (6 oz/185 g)

**Feta cheese,** ½ lb (250 g), crumbled

**Green (spring) onions,** 8, thinly sliced

SERVES 4

# curried chicken salad

**Salt and white pepper**

**Skinless, boneless chicken breasts,** 1 ½ lb (750 g)

**Mayonnaise,** 1 cup
(8 fl oz/250 ml)

**Curry powder,** 2 teaspoons

**Honey,** 1 tablespoon

**White wine vinegar,**
1 tablespoon

**Celery,** 4 stalks, chopped

**Apples such as Fuji, Gala, or Granny Smith,** 3, cored and cut into small cubes

**Pecan halves,** 1 cup
(4 oz/125 g), toasted

**Butter (Boston) lettuce,**
1 head, pale inner leaves only

SERVES 4

1 **Poach the chicken**
Bring a large saucepan of water to a boil over high heat. Add ½ teaspoon salt and the chicken, reduce the heat until the water is barely simmering, and cook until opaque throughout, 8–10 minutes. Remove from the heat and let stand until cool enough to handle. Cut the chicken into bite-sized cubes.

2 **Make the dressing**
Meanwhile, in a large bowl, whisk together the mayonnaise, curry powder, honey, vinegar, ½ teaspoon salt, and a pinch of pepper until smooth.

3 **Assemble the salad**
Add the chicken, celery, apples, and half of the pecans to the dressing and toss to coat evenly. Arrange the lettuce on plates and top with the chicken mixture. Sprinkle with the remaining pecans and serve.

## cook's tip

You can save time by using
a purchased rotisserie chicken.
Remove and discard the skin
from the chicken, then pull the
white and dark meat from
the bones. Cut the meat into
cubes or bite-sized pieces.
You will need about 4 cups
(1½ lb/750 g).

**ook's tip**

ek out the freshest ahi
na you can find. Purchase
eaks that are at least
inch (2.5 cm) thick.
aring for 1½ minutes

er side will result in steaks
hat are browned on the
utside but still pink in
he center. If you prefer to
:ook your tuna to medium,
ear the steaks for about
2 minutes longer per side.

# seared tuna with asian slaw

### 1 Make the dressing

In a large bowl, whisk together the ginger, mayonnaise, mustard, soy sauce, vinegar, sesame oil, and 5 tablespoons (2½ fl oz/75 ml) of the peanut oil until smooth.

### 2 Sear the tuna

Prepare a gas or charcoal grill for direct grilling over high heat. Alternatively, preheat a stovetop grill pan over high heat. Brush both sides of the tuna steaks with the remaining 2 tablespoons peanut oil and season generously with salt and pepper. Place the tuna on the grill rack or in the grill pan and sear without moving the steaks for 1½ minutes. Turn and sear for 1½ minutes longer, again without moving the steaks. Transfer to a cutting board and let stand for 5 minutes.

### 3 Assemble the salad

Meanwhile, add the cabbage, green onions, and bell peppers to the dressing and toss to coat evenly. Arrange the cabbage mixture on plates. Slice the tuna steaks across the grain, place on top of the salads, and serve.

**Ginger,** 1 teaspoon grated

**Mayonnaise,** 1 tablespoon

**Honey Dijon mustard,** 2 teaspoons

**Soy sauce,** 1 tablespoon

**Rice vinegar,** ¼ cup (2 fl oz/60 ml)

**Asian sesame oil,** 2 tablespoons

**Peanut oil,** 7 tablespoons (3½ fl oz/105 ml)

**Sushi-grade ahi tuna steaks,** 1½ lb (750 g), patted dry

**Salt and freshly ground pepper**

**Napa cabbage,** 1 large head, halved, cored, and thinly sliced crosswise

**Green (spring) onions,** 6, thinly sliced

**Red bell peppers (capsicums),** 2, seeded and thinly sliced

SERVES 4–6

29

# polenta, tomato & corn salad

**Diced tomatoes,** 1 can
(15 oz/470 g), drained

**Lemon juice,** from ½ lemon

**Curry powder,** ¾ teaspoon

**Olive oil,** 4 tablespoons
(2 fl oz/60 ml)

**Corn kernels,** from 1 ear
of corn (about 1 cup/6 oz/
185 g)

**Salt and freshly ground
pepper**

**Canola oil,** 2 tablespoons

**Precooked polenta tube,**
17 oz (530 g), cut into 8 slices

**Frisée or arugula (rocket),**
6 oz (185 g), torn into bite-
sized pieces

SERVES 4

### 1 Make the tomato-corn mixture

In a small saucepan over medium-low heat, combine the tomatoes, lemon juice, curry powder, and 2 tablespoons of the olive oil, and cook, stirring, until warm throughout, about 5 minutes. Stir in the corn, season to taste with salt, and remove from the heat.

### 2 Fry the polenta

In a large frying pan over medium heat, warm the canola oil. Season the polenta slices on both sides with salt and pepper. Add the slices to the pan and cook, turning once, until golden on both sides, about 8 minutes total. Transfer to paper towels and drain briefly.

### 3 Assemble the salad

In a large bowl, combine the frisée and the remaining 2 tablespoons olive oil and toss to coat evenly. Season to taste with salt and pepper. Arrange the polenta slices on plates, top with the tomato-corn mixture and the frisée, and serve.

## cook's tip

If you can't find precooked polenta, you can make your own using instant polenta. Prepare according to package directions, then pour onto a rimmed baking sheet. Smooth the top and let set, uncovered, for at least 1 hour or covered and refrigerated for up to overnight. Slice into rectangles or cut out 2-inch (5-cm) rounds using a biscuit cutter and panfry as directed.

# antipasto
## salad

### 1 Cook the vegetables

Prepare a gas or charcoal grill for direct grilling over high heat. Alternatively, preheat the broiler (grill). In a shallow dish, combine the zucchini and eggplant slices, ¼ cup oil, and garlic. Toss to coat and season generously with salt and pepper. Place the zucchini and eggplant on the grill rack and cook, turning once, until tender and golden, about 3 minutes per side. Or, arrange the slices on a rimmed baking sheet and place in the broiler. Cook, turning once, for about 3 minutes per side.

### 2 Assemble the platter

Place the olives in a small bowl and set on a large platter. Cut the grilled vegetables crosswise into bite-sized pieces and arrange on the platter. Arrange the tomato and mozzarella slices on the platter, overlapping them, then sprinkle with the basil and drizzle with the 1 tablespoon oil. Fan out the salami and prosciutto slices, top with the bell peppers, and serve.

**Zucchini (courgettes),** 4 small, cut lengthwise into thick slices

**Asian eggplants (slender aubergines),** 3, cut lengthwise into thick slices

**Olive oil,** ¼ cup (2 fl oz/ 60 ml), plus 1 tablespoon

**Garlic,** 2 cloves, minced

**Salt and freshly ground pepper**

**Assorted brine-cured olives,** 1½ cups (8 oz/250 g)

**Plum (Roma) tomatoes,** 4 small, cut into thick slices

**Fresh mozzarella cheese,** ½ lb (250 g), thickly sliced

**Fresh basil,** 2 tablespoons finely shredded

**Dry salami or *coppa*,** ¼ lb (125 g), sliced

**Prosciutto,** ¼ lb (125 g), thinly sliced

**Jarred roasted red bell peppers (capsicums),** 2, cut into strips

SERVES 4–6

# halibut skewers with arugula salad

**Lemon juice,** from 1 lemon

**Dijon mustard,** 2 teaspoons

**Fresh tarragon,** 1 teaspoon minced

**Salt and freshly ground pepper**

**Olive oil,** 6 tablespoons (3 fl oz/90 ml), plus 1 tablespoon

**Halibut fillet,** 1 ¼ lb (625 g), cut into large cubes

**Zucchini (courgettes),** 4 small, halved lengthwise and thinly sliced crosswise

**Plum (Roma) tomatoes,** 4 small, cut into thin wedges

**Red onion,** ¼, cut into slivers

**Arugula (rocket),** ½ lb (250 g)

**Pine nuts,** ⅓ cup (2 oz/ 60 g), toasted

**SERVES 4**

### 1 Make the dressing

Prepare a gas or charcoal grill for direct grilling over high heat. Alternatively, preheat the broiler (grill). Soak 4 bamboo skewers in water until needed. In a bowl, whisk together the lemon juice, mustard, tarragon, ½ teaspoon salt, and a pinch of pepper. Gradually whisk in the 6 tablespoons oil until smooth.

### 2 Cook the halibut

Thread the halibut on the soaked skewers. Brush with the 1 tablespoon oil and season all sides with salt and pepper. Place the skewers on the grill rack and cook, turning occasionally with tongs, until the halibut is opaque throughout, about 5 minutes. Or, arrange the skewers on a rimmed baking sheet and place in the broiler. Cook, turning occasionally, for 5–6 minutes total.

### 3 Assemble the salad

Add the zucchini, tomatoes, onion, arugula, and pine nuts to the dressing and toss to coat evenly. Arrange on plates, top with the skewers of halibut, and serve.

## cook's tip

Toast pine nuts in a dry nonstick
frying pan over medium-low heat,
shaking the pan frequently, for
about 5 minutes. Or, spread them
evenly on a baking sheet and
place in a 350°F (180°C) oven
for 10–12 minutes. The nuts are
done when they are golden.

## cook's tip

Goat cheese is much easier to cut when it is very cold, rather than at room temperature. If the cold cheese is still difficult to cut, dip a sharp knife in hot water and then dry it with a paper towel. Warm and dry the knife before cutting each slice.

# warm goat cheese & chicken salad

1 **Coat the goat cheese**
In a shallow bowl, combine the bread crumbs and a pinch each of salt and pepper. Lightly beat the egg in another shallow bowl. Dip 1 flat surface of each goat cheese round into the egg, letting the excess egg drip back into the bowl. Then dip in the bread crumbs, patting the crumbs in place. Repeat with the other flat surface of each goat cheese round, leaving the rims of the rounds uncoated.

2 **Make the dressing**
In a large bowl, whisk together the lemon zest and juice, mustard, ¼ teaspoon salt, and a pinch of pepper. Gradually whisk in the olive oil until smooth. Stir in the tarragon.

3 **Assemble the salad and cook the goat cheese**
Add the mixed greens and the chicken to the dressing and toss to coat evenly. Arrange on plates. In a large nonstick frying pan over medium-high heat, warm the canola oil until it shimmers. Working in batches if necessary, add the goat cheese rounds and cook until just beginning to soften but not melt, about 45 seconds. Carefully turn the rounds and cook for about 30 seconds longer. Transfer to the plates and serve.

**Fine dried bread crumbs or *panko*,** ½ cup (2 oz/60 g)

**Salt and freshly ground pepper**

**Egg,** 1

**Fresh goat cheese,** ½ lb (250 g), cut into 8 thick rounds

**Lemon zest and juice,** from 1 lemon

**Dijon or tarragon mustard,** 1 teaspoon

**Olive oil,** 5 tablespoons (2½ fl oz/75 ml)

**Fresh tarragon,** 2 teaspoons finely chopped

**Mixed baby salad greens,** 6 oz (185 g)

**Cooked chicken, poached (page 26) or rotisserie,** 3 cups (18 oz/560 g) shredded

**Canola oil,** 2 tablespoons

**SERVES 4**

# 30 minutes
# start to finish

# roast chicken & bread salad

**Garlic,** 1 clove, minced

**Balsamic vinegar,** 1½ tablespoons

**Dijon mustard,** 1 tablespoon

**Salt and freshly ground pepper**

**Olive oil,** ⅓ cup (3 fl oz/ 80 ml), plus ¼ cup (2 fl oz/ 60 ml)

**Day-old French or Italian bread,** 4 or 5 thick slices, crusts removed and cut into cubes (about 4 cups/ 8 oz/250 g)

**Baby spinach,** 6 oz (185 g)

**Pine nuts,** ⅓ cup (2 oz/ 60 g), toasted (page 35)

**Dried currants,** ½ cup (3 oz/90 g)

**Rotisserie chicken,** 1, about 3 lb (1.5 kg), cut into 8 serving pieces

**SERVES 4**

### 1 Make the vinaigrette

In a large bowl, whisk together the garlic, vinegar, mustard, ½ teaspoon salt, and a pinch of pepper. Gradually whisk in the ⅓ cup oil until smooth.

### 2 Make the croutons

In a large frying pan over medium-high heat, warm the ¼ cup oil. Add the bread cubes, toss to coat evenly, and cook, turning with tongs, until golden on all sides, about 5 minutes. Season to taste with salt and pepper and immediately transfer to the bowl with the vinaigrette.

### 3 Assemble the salad

Working quickly, add the spinach, pine nuts, and currants to the croutons and toss to coat evenly. Arrange on plates. Top each salad with 2 pieces of chicken and serve.

## cook's tip

Use a sharp chef's knife or poultry shears to divide a rotisserie chicken into serving pieces. Cut each breast crosswise into 2 pieces, keeping the wing attached. Remove each thigh from the body along with as much meat from the backbone as possible, then separate the drumstick from the thigh. Reserve the backbone for making stock.

# warm escarole, egg & bacon salad

### 1 Make the vinaigrette

Bring a small saucepan of water to a boil. Add the bacon and cook for 5 minutes. Drain, transfer to paper towels, and blot dry. Dry the saucepan, place over medium-low heat, and add the oil, garlic, and bacon. Cook, stirring occasionally, until the garlic is golden and the bacon is crisp, about 3 minutes. Be careful not to let the garlic burn. Remove from the heat and discard the garlic. Stir in the mustard and 2 tablespoons vinegar.

### 2 Poach the eggs

Choose a large, wide pan with a tight-fitting lid. Fill with a generous amount of water, add the 1 teaspoon vinegar, place over high heat, and bring to a rolling boil. Turn off the heat. Working quickly, crack each egg and release it just above the surface of the water, letting it ease into the water and spacing the eggs evenly. Immediately cover the pan and let the eggs stand undisturbed for 3–4 minutes, depending on how runny you prefer the yolks.

### 3 Assemble the salads

Place the escarole in a large bowl. Bring the vinaigrette to a boil. Pour over the escarole and immediately toss to wilt the leaves slightly. Season to taste with salt and pepper. Toss again and arrange on plates. Using a slotted spoon, transfer a poached egg to the top of each salad and serve.

**Thick-cut bacon,** 4 slices, chopped

**Olive oil,** ¼ cup (2 fl oz/ 60 ml)

**Garlic,** 1 clove, bruised

**Whole-grain mustard,** 1 tablespoon

**Red wine vinegar,** 2 tablespoons, plus 1 teaspoon

**Eggs,** 4

**Escarole (Batavian endive),** 2 heads, tough outer leaves removed, torn into bite-sized pieces

**Salt and freshly ground pepper**

SERVES 4

# moroccan couscous salad

**Olive oil,** ¼ cup (2 fl oz/ 60 ml), plus 2 tablespoons

**Yellow onion,** 1, finely chopped

**Garlic,** 2 cloves, minced

**Chicken broth,** 2¾ cups (22 fl oz/680 ml)

**Salt and freshly ground pepper**

**Instant couscous,** 1½ cups (9 oz/280 g)

**Slivered almonds,** ¾ cup (3 oz/90 g)

**Chickpeas (garbanzo beans),** 1 can (15 oz/470 g), rinsed and drained

**Red bell pepper (capsicum),** 1, seeded and chopped

**Brine-cured black olives,** ¾ cup (3½ oz/105 g), pitted and chopped

**Lemon juice,** from 1 lemon

**Fresh flat-leaf (Italian) parsley,** ¼ cup (⅓ oz/10 g) finely chopped

SERVES 4

1 Prepare the couscous
In a large saucepan over medium-low heat, warm 1 tablespoon of the oil. Add the onion and cook, stirring occasionally, until softened, about 4 minutes. Add the garlic and cook for 1 minute longer. Add the broth, ½ teaspoon salt, and several grinds of pepper and bring to a boil. Place the couscous in a large stainless-steel bowl and pour the hot liquid over it. Blend well with a fork, cover with a plate, and let stand for 5 minutes.

2 Toast the almonds
Meanwhile, in a large frying pan over medium heat, warm 1 tablespoon of the oil. Add the almonds and toast, stirring, until crisp and golden, 5–7 minutes. Transfer to a plate.

3 Assemble the salad
Fluff the couscous with a fork. Add the toasted almonds, chickpeas, bell pepper, olives, lemon juice, parsley, and ¼ cup oil to the couscous. Toss gently to combine. Taste, adjust the seasoning with salt and pepper, and serve.

## cook's tip

Couscous, often mistakenly called a grain, is actually a pasta made up of tiny pearls of wheat dough. To save time, purchase instant couscous, which has been presteamed and is ready in only a few minutes once combined with hot liquid.

# grilled asparagus & prosciutto salad

## 1 Grill the asparagus

Prepare a gas or charcoal grill for direct grilling over medium-high heat. Alternatively, preheat a stovetop grill pan over medium-high heat. Brush the asparagus with 1 tablespoon of the oil and season with salt and pepper. Place the spears on the grill rack or in the grill pan and cook, turning occasionally with tongs, until slightly charred and tender, about 8 minutes.

## 2 Make the vinaigrette

In a large bowl, whisk together the garlic, vinegar, mustard, ¼ teaspoon salt, and a pinch of pepper. Gradually whisk in the remaining 6 tablespoons (3 fl oz/90 ml) oil until smooth. Stir in the chives.

## 3 Assemble the salad

Add the greens and prosciutto to the vinaigrette and toss to coat evenly. Arrange the asparagus on plates and top with the greens. Top with the Parmesan, if using, and serve.

**Asparagus,** 1¼ lb (625 g), tough bases trimmed

**Olive oil,** 7 tablespoons (3½ fl oz/105 ml)

**Salt and freshly ground pepper**

**Garlic,** 1 clove, minced

**Red wine vinegar,** 2 tablespoons

**Tarragon or Dijon mustard,** 1 teaspoon

**Fresh chives,** 1 tablespoon finely snipped

**Mixed baby greens,** 6 oz (185 g)

**Prosciutto,** 3 oz (90 g), thinly sliced and cut into strips

**Parmesan cheese,** 2 oz (60 g), shaved (optional)

SERVES 4

# grilled chicken caesar

**Mayonnaise,** 1 tablespoon

**Garlic,** 2 cloves, minced

**Anchovy fillets,** 1–3, finely chopped (optional)

**Dijon mustard,** 2 teaspoons

**Lemon juice,** from 1 lemon

**Worcestershire sauce,** 1 teaspoon

**Red wine vinegar,** 1 teaspoon

**Olive oil,** 5 tablespoons (2½ fl oz/75 ml)

**Salt and freshly ground pepper**

**Skinless, boneless chicken breasts,** 1¼ lb (625 g), pounded lightly to an even thickness

**Romaine (cos) lettuce,** 3 heads, pale inner leaves only

**Parmesan cheese,** 3 oz (90 g), shaved

SERVES 4

### 1 Make the dressing

In a blender, combine the mayonnaise, garlic, anchovies to taste, if using, mustard, lemon juice, Worcestershire sauce, vinegar, 4 tablespoons (2 fl oz/60 ml) of the oil, ½ teaspoon salt, and a generous amount of pepper. Process until smooth.

### 2 Grill the chicken

Prepare a gas or charcoal grill for direct grilling over high heat. Alternatively, preheat a stovetop grill pan over high heat. Brush both sides of the chicken breasts with the remaining 1 tablespoon oil and season generously with salt and pepper. Place the chicken on the grill rack or in the grill pan and cook, turning once, until opaque throughout, 4–5 minutes per side. Transfer to a cutting board and let stand for 5–7 minutes. Cut on the diagonal into slices.

### 3 Assemble the salad

Meanwhile, in a large bowl, combine the lettuce and dressing and toss to coat evenly. Arrange the lettuce on plates, top with the chicken slices and Parmesan, and serve.

## cook's tip

Pounding boneless chicken breasts lightly helps them to cook more evenly. Place 1 breast between 2 sheets of wax paper or plastic wrap and pound gently 3 or 4 times with a metal meat pounder or the base of a small saucepan to an even thickness. Repeat for the remaining breasts.

## cook's tip

If the salmon fillet still has its skin,
you don't need to spend time
removing it before you cook the
salmon. The skin will protect
the delicate flesh during steaming.
After cooking, the salmon flesh
will flake easily away from the
skin, which can then be discarded.

# salmon
# & fennel salad

### 1 Poach the salmon

Season both sides of the salmon with salt and pepper. Lightly oil a steamer rack and place in a saucepan. Fill the pan with water to just below the base of the steamer rack and bring to a simmer. Add the salmon, cover, and cook until opaque throughout, about 10 minutes per 1 inch (2.5 cm) of thickness. Transfer to a plate. Let cool slightly, then flake with a fork into large chunks, discarding any skin and errant bones.

### 2 Make the vinaigrette

In a large bowl, whisk together the lemon zest and juice, vinegar, mustard, ½ teaspoon salt, a pinch of pepper, and half of the chives. Gradually whisk in the oil until smooth.

### 3 Assemble the salad

Place the fennel quarters, cut side down, and slice crosswise as thinly as possible. Add to the vinaigrette and toss to coat evenly. Add the greens and salmon and toss to combine. Arrange on plates, sprinkle with the remaining chives, and serve.

**Salmon fillet,** 1 lb (500 g)

**Salt and freshly ground pepper**

**Lemon zest,** from 1 lemon, finely grated

**Lemon juice,** from 1 lemon

**Champagne or white wine vinegar,** 1 tablespoon

**Dijon mustard,** 2 teaspoons

**Fresh chives,** 2 tablespoons finely snipped

**Olive oil,** 6 tablespoons (3 fl oz/90 ml)

**Fennel bulbs,** 2, trimmed, quartered lengthwise, and cored

**Mixed baby greens,** 6 oz (185 g)

SERVES 4

# sausages with warm cabbage salad

**Savoy cabbage,** 1 small head, cored and thinly sliced

**Salt and freshly ground black pepper**

**Smoked pork or chicken sausages,** 4, 1½ lb (750 g) total weight

**Olive oil,** ¾ cup (6 fl oz/ 180 ml)

**Red onion,** 1 small, finely chopped

**Sherry vinegar,** 3 tablespoons

**Whole-grain mustard,** 2 tablespoons

**Red pepper flakes,** ¼ teaspoon

**Red bell pepper (capsicum),** 1, seeded, quartered, and thinly sliced crosswise

SERVES 4

1 **Cook the cabbage and sausages**
Bring a large saucepan of water to a boil. Add the cabbage and 1½ teaspoons salt and cook until the cabbage is slightly wilted, about 3 minutes. Drain, rinse under running cold water, and drain well. Preheat the broiler (grill) and place the rack at the highest level. Using a sharp knife, lightly score the sausages. Arrange the sausages on a rimmed baking sheet and broil (grill), turning occasionally, until the skin is crisp, about 6 minutes. Transfer to a cutting board and let stand for 5 minutes. Cut into slices ½ inch (12 mm) thick.

2 **Make the dressing**
Meanwhile, in a small saucepan over medium heat, combine the oil and onion. Bring to a gentle simmer and cook until the onion is tender, about 7 minutes. Add the vinegar, mustard, red pepper flakes, ¾ teaspoon salt, and a generous amount of pepper. Stir to combine.

3 **Assemble the salad**
In a large bowl, combine the cabbage and bell pepper. Quickly pour the hot dressing over the vegetables and toss until the cabbage is tender and has begun to lose some of its volume, 1–2 minutes. Arrange on plates, top with the sliced sausages, and serve.

## cook's tip

For this dish, use spicy smoked
sausages made from chicken,
pork, or turkey, such as andouille,
hot Italian, or even chorizo. Other
German-style sausages, such
as bratwurst, could also be used.

# grilled summer vegetable salad

## 1 Grill the vegetables

Prepare a gas or charcoal grill for direct grilling over high heat. Alternatively, preheat the broiler (grill). Place the eggplant and squash slices in a shallow dish and brush both sides with the 3 tablespoons oil. Season with salt and pepper and the oregano. Place the slices on the grill rack and cook, turning once, until tender and golden, 2–3 minutes. Or, arrange the slices on a rimmed baking sheet and place in the broiler. Cook, turning once, for 2–3 minutes per side.

## 2 Make the vinaigrette

In a large bowl, whisk together the vinegar, mustard, ¼ teaspoon salt, and a pinch of pepper. Gradually whisk in the ¼ cup oil until smooth.

## 3 Assemble the salad

Cut the grilled vegetables into bite-sized pieces and add to the vinaigrette. Add the tomatoes and greens. Toss to coat well, sprinkle with the cheese, and serve.

**Eggplant (aubergine),** 1 large or 2 small, cut lengthwise into thick slices

**Yellow summer squash such as crookneck or yellow zucchini (courgettes),** 3, cut lengthwise into thick slices

**Olive oil,** ¼ cup (2 fl oz/ 60 ml), plus 3 tablespoons

**Salt and freshly ground pepper**

**Dried oregano,** ½ teaspoon

**Balsamic vinegar,** 1 tablespoon

**Dijon mustard,** 1 teaspoon

**Tomatoes,** 4, cored and quartered

**Mixed baby greens,** 3 oz (90 g)

**Fresh goat cheese,** ⅔ cup (3 oz/90 g) crumbled

SERVES 4

# arugula, squash & salami salad

**Garlic,** 1 clove, sliced

**Fresh flat-leaf (Italian) parsley leaves,** ¾ cup (¾ oz/20 g) firmly packed

**Fresh mint leaves,** ¼ cup (¼ oz/7 g) firmly packed

**Capers,** 2 teaspoons, rinsed and drained

**Dijon mustard,** 1 teaspoon

**Red wine vinegar,** 3 teaspoons

**Olive oil,** ¼ cup (2 fl oz/ 60 ml), plus 2 tablespoons

**Butternut squash,** 1 lb (500 g), halved, seeded, peeled, and cut into cubes

**Salt and freshly ground pepper**

**Arugula (rocket),** ½ lb (250 g)

**Salami,** ¼ lb (125 g), cut into thin strips

**Pine nuts,** 2 tablespoons, toasted (page 35)

**SERVES 4**

1 **Make the salsa verde**
In a blender, combine the garlic, parsley, mint, capers, Dijon mustard, 1 teaspoon of the vinegar, and the ¼ cup oil. Process until smooth.

2 **Roast the squash**
Preheat the oven to 500°F (260°C). On a rimmed baking sheet, toss the squash with 1 tablespoon of the oil, season generously with salt and pepper, and spread in an even layer. Roast, shaking the pan vigorously every 5 minutes, until the squash is tender, about 15 minutes. Let cool in the pan for 5 minutes. Add the *salsa verde* and toss gently to coat evenly.

3 **Assemble the salad**
In a large bowl, combine the arugula, salami, remaining 1 tablespoon oil, ¼ teaspoon salt, and a pinch of pepper. Toss to combine, add the remaining 2 teaspoons vinegar, and toss again. Arrange on plates and top with the squash. Sprinkle with the pine nuts and serve.

## cook's tip

The *salsa verde* can be made up to 4 hours ahead of time. Keep it covered and refrigerated until just before serving to preserve the color. You can roast the squash up to 1 hour ahead. Keep it at room temperature and toss with the *salsa verde* just before serving.

## cook's tip

The ingredients that you add to a pasta salad can be as varied as the shapes of pasta that you use. Replace the crab, shrimp, and asparagus in this recipe with shredded, poached chicken (page 26) and thawed petite peas or experiment with your own combinations of meat, poultry, or seafood and vegetables.

# pasta salad with crab & shrimp

**1 Cook the pasta and asparagus**
Bring a large pot of water to a boil. Add 2 tablespoons salt and the pasta. Cook, stirring occasionally to prevent sticking, until the pasta is al dente, according to the package directions. About 4 minutes before the pasta is finished cooking, add the asparagus to the boiling water and cook until tender-crisp. Drain the pasta and asparagus, rinse under cold running water, and drain again.

**2 Make the dressing**
Meanwhile, in a large bowl, whisk together the garlic, vinegar, mustard, mayonnaise, ½ teaspoon salt, and a pinch of pepper. Gradually whisk in the oil until smooth. Add the pasta and asparagus to the dressing and toss to coat evenly.

**3 Assemble the salad**
Add the crabmeat (breaking it up slightly), shrimp, and tarragon to the pasta and toss to combine. Arrange the lettuce on plates, top with the pasta salad, and serve.

**Salt and freshly ground pepper**

**Penne, fusilli, or tubetti,** ¾ lb (375 g)

**Asparagus,** 1 bunch, about 1 ½ lb (750 g), tough ends trimmed and spears cut into pieces

**Garlic,** 1 clove, minced

**Balsamic vinegar,** 3 tablespoons

**Dijon mustard,** 1 teaspoon

**Mayonnaise,** 2 tablespoons

**Olive oil,** ¼ cup (2 fl oz/ 60 ml)

**Fresh lump crabmeat,** ¼ lb (125 g), picked over for shell fragments

**Cooked small shrimp (prawns),** ¼ lb (125 g)

**Fresh tarragon,** 2 teaspoons finely chopped

**Green- or red-leaf lettuce,** 1 small head, torn into bite-sized pieces

SERVES 4

59

# niçoise salad
## with salmon

**Shallot,** 1, minced

**Red wine vinegar,** 3 tablespoons

**Dijon mustard,** 1 tablespoon

**Salt and freshly ground pepper**

**Olive oil,** ½ cup (4 fl oz/ 125 ml), plus 2 tablespoons

**Small boiling potatoes,** about 15, quartered

**Slender green beans,** ½ lb (250 g), trimmed

**Salmon fillet,** 1½ lb (750 g), cut crosswise into 4 equal slices

**Belgian endive (chicory/ witloof),** 4 large or 6 small heads, ends trimmed and cut lengthwise into slivers

**Hard-boiled eggs,** 4, quartered

**Anchovy fillets,** 8–12, soaked for 5 minutes in warm water and patted dry (optional)

**Niçoise olives,** ¼ cup (2 oz/60 g), pitted

SERVES 4

1 **Make the vinaigrette**
In a large bowl, whisk together the shallot, vinegar, mustard, ¼ teaspoon salt, and a pinch of pepper. Gradually whisk in the ½ cup oil until smooth.

2 **Cook the vegetables**
Bring a large saucepan of water to a boil. Add the potatoes and 1 tablespoon salt and cook until tender, about 7 minutes. Add the green beans during the last 3 minutes of cooking. Drain the vegetables, rinse under running cold water until no longer warm, and drain again. Add to the vinaigrette and toss to coat evenly.

3 **Sear the salmon and assemble the salad**
Preheat a large frying pan over high heat. Brush both sides of the salmon slices with the 2 tablespoons oil and season generously with salt and pepper. Place the salmon in the hot pan and sear without moving the slices for about 2 minutes. Turn and sear again without moving for about 2 minutes longer. Reduce the heat to medium and cook, turning once, until firm to the touch but still slightly pink on the inside, 2–4 minutes longer. Transfer to a plate. Add the endive to the bowl with the vegetables and toss to coat with the vinaigrette. Arrange on plates. Place a slice of salmon in the center of each salad. Arrange the eggs, anchovies (if using), and olives over and around the salads, and serve.

## cook's tip

For a faster and easier sal that is closer to the classic version of Niçoise, replace the seared salmon with the highest-quality canned

tuna that you can find, preferably packed in olive oil. If available, try one of the large cans of flavorful imported tuna packed in olive oil from Spain or Italy, which can be found at well-stocked markets.

## cook's tip

Salty and rustic manchego, a traditional aged sheep's milk cheese, is so popular that it is regarded as the national cheese of Spain. It is widely available, but if you are unable to find it, an aged pecorino or Parmesan cheese may be substituted.

# grilled
# portobello salad

### 1 Grill the mushrooms

Prepare a gas or charcoal grill for direct grilling over medium-high heat. Alternatively, preheat the broiler (grill). Brush both sides of the mushrooms with the 3 tablespoons oil and season generously with salt and pepper. Place the mushrooms, gill side down, on the grill rack and cook for about 8 minutes. Transfer to a plate, rounded sides down, and sprinkle with the garlic and vinegar. Return to the grill, rounded side down, and cook until crisp on the outside and softened on the inside, about 10 minutes longer. Or, arrange the mushrooms on a rimmed baking sheet and place in the broiler. Cook, using the same seasoning and timing as for grilling.

### 2 Make the vinaigrette

Meanwhile, in a large bowl, whisk together the lemon juice, thyme, $1/4$ teaspoon salt, and a pinch of pepper. Gradually whisk in the $1/4$ cup oil until smooth.

### 3 Assemble the salad

Cut the warm mushrooms into thin slices. Add the lettuce and pears to the vinaigrette, toss to coat evenly, and arrange on plates. Top with the mushroom slices, sprinkle with the cheese, and serve.

**Portobello mushrooms,** 4 large, stems removed

**Olive oil,** $1/4$ cup (2 fl oz/ 60 ml), plus 3 tablespoons

**Salt and freshly ground pepper**

**Garlic,** 2 cloves, minced

**Balsamic vinegar,** 2 teaspoons

**Lemon juice,** from 1 lemon

**Fresh thyme,** $1/2$ teaspoon minced

**Romaine (cos) lettuce,** 3 heads, pale inner leaves only, torn into bite-sized pieces

**Pears,** 3, peeled, halved, cored, and cut into thin wedges

**Manchego cheese,** 2 oz (60 g), shaved

**SERVES 4**

# vietnamese shrimp & noodle salad

**Dried rice stick noodles,**
½ lb (250 g)

**Lemongrass,** 2 stalks, pale inner core only, finely minced

**Fresh ginger,** 2 tablespoons finely grated

**Lime juice,** from 1 lime

**Asian fish sauce,**
3 tablespoons

**Asian sesame oil,**
2 teaspoons, plus
1 tablespoon

**Sugar,** 1 teaspoon

**Small shrimp (prawns),**
1 lb (500 g), peeled and deveined

**Green (spring) onions,** 12, thinly sliced

**Fresh mint,** ¼ cup (⅓ oz/ 10 g) coarsely chopped

**Romaine (cos) lettuce,**
1 head, pale inner leaves only, torn into bite-sized pieces

**Roasted peanuts,** ½ cup (2½ oz/75 g), chopped

SERVES 4

1 **Soak the noodles and make the dressing**
In a large bowl, soak the rice stick noodles in hot water to cover for 15 minutes. Drain. Meanwhile, in another bowl, whisk together the lemongrass, ginger, lime juice, fish sauce, 2 teaspoons sesame oil, and sugar.

2 **Cook the noodles**
Bring a large pot of water to a boil. Plunge the reconstituted noodles into the water for 5 seconds and drain immediately. Rinse well under running cold water, and drain again. Add to the dressing and toss to coat evenly.

3 **Cook the shrimp and assemble the salad**
In a frying pan over medium-high heat, warm the remaining 1 tablespoon sesame oil. Add the shrimp and cook, stirring frequently, until opaque throughout, 2–3 minutes. Add the shrimp, onions, and mint to the noodles and toss to combine. Arrange the lettuce on plates and top with the noodle mixture. Sprinkle with the peanuts and serve.

## cook's tip

When using lemongrass, be sure to cut off the grassy top and trim the root end of the stalk, then peel away the tough outer layers from the bulblike base. If you are unable to find fresh lemongrass, substitute the finely grated zest and the juice of 1 lemon.

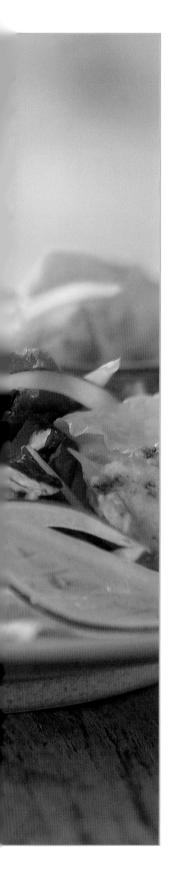

# fried chicken
## salad

### 1 Make the vinaigrette

In a large bowl, whisk together the mustard, vinegar, and 1 teaspoon salt. Gradually whisk in the olive oil until smooth.

### 2 Fry the chicken

Preheat the oven to 200°F (95°C). In a deep, heavy saucepan or Dutch oven over high heat, pour in canola oil to a depth of ½ inch (12 mm). Line a large baking sheet with a double layer of newspaper and place in the oven. In a large, resealable bag, combine the flour and 1½ teaspoons each salt and pepper, and the garlic powder, if using. Pour the buttermilk into a shallow bowl. When the oil reaches 360°F (182°C) on a deep-frying thermometer, dip the chicken pieces in the buttermilk. Remove, letting any excess drip back into the bowl, and place in the flour. Seal the bag and toss until the chicken is evenly coated. Using tongs, add half of the chicken to the hot oil and fry, turning occasionally, until golden and opaque throughout, 2–4 minutes. Using the tongs, transfer to the lined baking sheet and keep warm in the oven. Let the oil return to 360°F before frying the second batch.

### 3 Assemble the salad

Add the lettuce, tomato, onion, and pecans to the vinaigrette and toss to coat evenly. Arrange on plates, top with the chicken, and serve.

**Honey Dijon mustard,** 1 tablespoon

**Red wine vinegar,** 1 tablespoon

**Salt and freshly ground pepper**

**Olive oil,** ½ cup (4 fl oz/ 125 ml)

**Canola oil,** for frying

**Flour,** 1 cup (5 oz/155 g)

**Garlic powder,** 1½ teaspoons (optional)

**Buttermilk,** 1 cup (8 fl oz/250 ml)

**Skinless, boneless chicken breasts,** 1 lb (500 g), cut into large bite-sized pieces

**Romaine (cos) lettuce,** 1 head, pale inner leaves only, torn into bite-sized pieces

**Tomato,** 1 large, cut into bite-sized chunks

**Red onion,** 1 small, halved and cut into thin slivers

**Pecan halves,** 1 cup (4 oz/125 g), coarsely chopped

**SERVES 4**

67

15 minutes
hands-on time

# vietnamese beef & watercress salad

**Garlic,** 6 cloves, minced

**Asian fish sauce,** 2 teaspoons

**Sugar,** 1 teaspoon

**Salt and freshly ground pepper**

**Olive oil,** 3 tablespoons

**Sirloin steak,** 1¼ lb (625 g), trimmed of excess fat and cut into cubes

**Red onion,** 1 small, halved and very thinly sliced

**Rice vinegar,** 2 tablespoons

**Canola oil,** 2 teaspoons

**Watercress,** 6 oz (185 g), tender leaves and stems only

**Fresh cilantro (fresh coriander) leaves,** 1 cup (1 oz/30 g) loosely packed

SERVES 4

1 **Marinate the beef**
In a resealable plastic bag, combine the garlic, fish sauce, sugar, ½ teaspoon salt, a pinch of pepper, and 2 tablespoons of the olive oil. Add the beef, seal the bag, and squeeze to distribute the ingredients. Let stand for 30 minutes at room temperature or up to 1½ hours in the refrigerator (return to room temperature before cooking).

2 **Marinate the onion**
In a bowl, toss the onion with the vinegar and season generously with pepper. Let stand for 10–15 minutes. Add the remaining 1 tablespoon olive oil and toss to combine.

3 **Assemble the salad and stir-fry the beef**
Place a wok or deep, heavy frying pan over high heat and add the canola oil. Meanwhile, arrange the watercress and cilantro on plates and top with the onion. When the oil is very hot, add the beef and the marinade and stir-fry until the beef is browned on all sides, 1½–2½ minutes. Do not overcook. Scatter the beef over the salads and serve.

## cook's tip

To keep your salad greens crisp, rinse the leaves in cold water, dry them in a salad spinner, wrap them in a kitchen towel, and refrigerate for at least 15 minutes before serving. This time in the refrigerator yields greens that are crisper than if spun dry just before serving.

# crab cake & butter lettuce salad

### 1 Prepare the crab cakes

In a bowl, whisk the eggs lightly. Add the 1 tablespoon mayonnaise, crab, bread crumbs, 2 teaspoons salt, ½ teaspoon pepper, and green onions. Stir with a fork until well mixed. Divide the mixture into 8 equal portions and gently form each portion into a small patty.

### 2 Make the dressing

In a small bowl, whisk together the ⅓ cup mayonnaise, mustard, lemon juice, and ¼ teaspoon pepper until smooth.

### 3 Cook the crab cakes and assemble the salad

In a large frying pan over medium-low heat, melt the butter. Working in batches if necessary, add the crab cakes and cook without moving them until golden brown on the first side, about 4 minutes. Turn and cook until golden brown on the second side, 3–4 minutes longer. Arrange the lettuce on plates and place the crab cakes alongside. Drizzle with the dressing and serve.

**Eggs,** 2

**Mayonnaise,** ⅓ cup (3 fl oz/ 80 ml), plus 1 tablespoon

**Fresh lump crabmeat,** 1 lb (500 g), picked over for shell fragments and squeezed to remove excess water

**Fine fresh white bread crumbs,** ½ cup (1 oz/30 g)

**Salt and freshly ground pepper**

**Green (spring) onions,** 4, finely chopped

**Dijon mustard,** 2 teaspoons

**Lemon juice,** from 1 lemon

**Unsalted butter,** 2 tablespoons

**Butter (Boston) lettuce,** 2 heads, torn into bite-sized pieces

SERVES 4

73

# mediterranean
# farro salad

**Farro,** 1 cup (5 oz/155 g)

**Lemon juice,** from 2 lemons

**Salt and freshly ground pepper**

**Olive oil,** ¼ cup (2 fl oz/ 60 ml)

**Radishes,** 8, thinly sliced

**English (hothouse) cucumber,** ½, peeled, halved lengthwise, and thinly sliced

**Fresh mint,** ⅓ cup (½ oz/ 15 g) loosely packed and then finely chopped

**Baby spinach,** 6 oz (185 g)

**Feta cheese,** 5 oz (155 g), crumbled

SERVES 4

### 1 Cook the farro

In a saucepan, combine the *farro* and 2 cups (16 fl oz/ 500 ml) water. Bring to a boil over high heat, then reduce the heat to low and simmer, covered, until the grains are plump and tender to the bite, about 30 minutes. Remove from the heat, uncover, and let cool slightly. (The *farro* can be prepared up to 1 day in advance and stored in the refrigerator.)

### 2 Make the vinaigrette

Meanwhile, in a large bowl, whisk together the lemon juice, ¼ teaspoon salt, and a pinch of pepper. Gradually whisk in the oil until smooth.

### 3 Assemble the salad

Add the radishes, cucumber, mint, and *farro* to the vinaigrette and toss to coat evenly. Gently toss in the spinach and feta and serve.

## cook's tip

*Farro*, an ancient grain, is available in Italian groceries, health-food stores, and most well-stocked markets. If you can't find *farro*, you can use bulgur instead. Place 1 cup (6 oz/185 g) bulgur in a large heatproof bowl and pour in 2 cups (16 fl oz/500 ml) boiling water. Let stand for 30 minutes, then fluff with a fork.

## cook's tip

Choose red, yellow-gold, Chiogga, or any other variety and/or color of beet for this bright salad. The beets may be prepared through Step 1, then covered and refrigerated overnight before continuing.

# beet, fennel & spinach salad

### 1 Cook the beets

Preheat the oven to 350°F (180°C). Wrap the beets separately in aluminum foil and bake until tender when pierced with a knife, 35–45 minutes. Let cool, then peel and cut into ½-inch (12-mm) cubes.

### 2 Make the vinaigrette

In a large bowl, whisk together the shallots, vinegar, orange zest and juice, coriander (if using), ½ teaspoon salt, and a pinch of pepper. Gradually whisk in the oil until smooth. Add the beets and toss to coat. Let stand at room temperature for about 30 minutes, stirring occasionally.

### 3 Assemble the salad

Add the fennel, spinach, and half of the cheese to the beets and toss to combine. Arrange on plates, top with the remaining cheese, and serve.

**Beets,** 4 small, stems trimmed but still intact

**Shallots,** 2, minced

**Balsamic vinegar,** 2 tablespoons

**Orange zest,** from ½ orange, finely grated

**Orange juice,** from ½ orange

**Ground coriander,** ½ teaspoon (optional)

**Salt and freshly ground pepper**

**Olive oil,** ¼ cup (2 fl oz/ 60 ml)

**Fennel,** 2 small bulbs or 1 large bulb, trimmed, quartered lengthwise, cored, and thinly sliced crosswise

**Baby spinach,** 5 oz (155 g)

**Ricotta salata or Parmesan cheese,** 1 oz (30 g), shaved

SERVES 4

# lentil, bacon & frisée salad

**Garlic,** 2 cloves, sliced

**Shallots,** 3, 1 sliced and 2 minced

**Sherry vinegar,** ¼ cup (2 fl oz/60 ml)

**Dijon mustard,** 1 tablespoon

**Olive oil,** ¾ cup (6 fl oz/ 180 ml)

**Salt and freshly ground pepper**

**Thick-cut bacon,** 4 slices, chopped

**Celery,** 1 stalk, finely chopped

**Carrot,** 1, finely chopped

**Dried French green lentils,** 2 cups (14 oz/440 g)

**Chicken broth,** 2 cups (16 fl oz/500 ml)

**Frisée,** 1 bunch, tough stems removed

SERVES 4

## 1 Make the vinaigrette and cook the bacon

In a blender, combine the garlic, sliced shallot, vinegar, mustard, oil, ¾ teaspoon salt, and ¼ teaspoon pepper. Process until smooth. (You will have more vinaigrette than you will need for the lentil salad; store the remainder in the refrigerator for up to 1 week.) In a large, heavy saucepan over low heat, cook the bacon, stirring occasionally, until crisp, about 8 minutes. Using a slotted spoon, transfer to paper towels to drain.

## 2 Cook the lentils

Return the saucepan to low heat, add the minced shallots to the bacon fat, and cook, stirring occasionally, until softened, about 4 minutes. Add the celery and carrot and cook, stirring occasionally, until wilted, 3–4 minutes. Add the lentils, broth, and enough water just to cover the lentils. Bring to a boil, reduce the heat to low, cover, and simmer gently until just tender but not yet mushy, about 20 minutes. Add a little more water if the lentils become too dry. Remove from the heat and let stand, covered, for 5 minutes. Immediately add half of the vinaigrette and toss to combine.

## 3 Assemble the salad

Scatter the frisée on plates and spoon the lentils over the top. Drizzle a little vinaigrette over the salads, sprinkle with the bacon, and serve.

## cook's tip

The remaining vinaigrette may be kept in an airtight container in the refrigerator for up to 1 week. This classic mustard vinaigrette

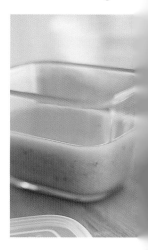

is extremely versatile. Make a double batch so you have it at the ready. Use it to drizzle over sliced tomatoes and avocado or toss with your favorite mixed baby salad greens.

## cook's tip

The potato salad may be prepared, without the chopped arugula (rocket), up to 1 day in advance. Cover and store in the refrigerator. Let the potato salad come to room temperature, then add the arugula just before serving.

# flank steak, arugula & potato salad

**1 Marinate the steak**
Place the flank steak on a large dish and brush both sides with 1 tablespoon of the oil. Season generously with salt and pepper and let stand for at least 1 hour at room temperature or up to 8 hours in the refrigerator (return to room temperature before cooking).

**2 Make the potato salad**
Place a steamer rack in a saucepan. Fill the pan with water to just below the base of the steamer rack and bring to a simmer. Add the potatoes, cover, and cook until just tender but not falling apart, 12–15 minutes. Drain and let cool. In a large bowl, whisk together the mustard, white wine vinegar, wine (if using), 3 tablespoons of the oil, ¼ teaspoon salt, and a pinch of pepper until smooth. Stir in the shallot and the chopped arugula. Add the potatoes and toss to coat evenly.

**3 Cook the steak and assemble the salad**
Preheat a large, heavy frying pan or grill pan over high heat. Add the steak and cook, turning once, 4–6 minutes per side for rare or medium-rare. Transfer to a cutting board and let stand for 5 minutes. Cut the steak across the grain into thin slices. Place the arugula leaves in a large bowl, drizzle with the remaining 2 tablespoons oil, and toss to coat evenly. Add ¼ teaspoon salt, a pinch of pepper, and the balsamic vinegar and toss again. Arrange the potato salad and warm steak slices on plates, top with the arugula, and serve.

**Flank steak,** 1¼ lb (625 g)

**Olive oil,** 6 tablespoons (3 fl oz/90 ml)

**Salt and freshly ground pepper**

**Small red potatoes,** 1 lb (500 g), quartered

**Dijon mustard,** 1 tablespoon

**White wine vinegar,** 1 tablespoon

**White wine or vermouth,** 2 teaspoons (optional)

**Shallot,** 1 large, minced

**Arugula (rocket),** 4 cups (4 oz/125 g) whole leaves, plus ½ cup (¾ oz/20 g) finely chopped

**Balsamic vinegar,** 2 teaspoons

SERVES 4

# mediterranean meze

**Eggplant (aubergine),** 1 large

**Garlic,** 1 clove, minced

**Ground cumin,** ¼ teaspoon

**Plain yogurt,** 1 tablespoon

**Lemon juice,** from 1 lemon

**Olive oil,** 3 tablespoons

**Fresh mint,** 2 tablespoons minced

**Salt and freshly ground pepper**

**English (hothouse) cucumber,** 1, peeled, halved lengthwise, and sliced

**Plum (Roma) tomatoes,** 4, cut into wedges

**Hummus,** ¾ lb (375 g)

**Tabbouleh,** 2½ cups (12 oz/375 g)

**Pita bread,** 8 rounds, each cut into 4 wedges, warmed

SERVES 4–6

1 **Make the eggplant spread**
Preheat the oven to 400°F (200°C). Prick the eggplant in several places with a fork and place in a roasting pan. Roast for 30 minutes. Turn the eggplant and continue to roast until the eggplant is very tender and slightly charred and the center has collapsed, about 30 minutes longer. Transfer to a colander set over a large bowl and let drain for 30 minutes. Scoop out the flesh into a bowl, discarding the skin and stem ends. Add the garlic, cumin, yogurt, lemon juice, 1 tablespoon of the oil, 1 tablespoon of the mint, ¼ teaspoon salt, and a pinch of pepper and mix well. Cover and refrigerate until the flavors have blended, about 1 hour.

2 **Make the cucumber-tomato salad**
In a bowl, combine the cucumber, tomatoes, remaining 1 tablespoon mint, remaining 2 tablespoons oil, and ¼ teaspoon salt. Toss to combine.

3 **Assemble the platter**
Transfer the eggplant spread, cucumber-tomato salad, hummus, and tabbouleh to individual bowls and place in the center of a large platter. Arrange the pita wedges around the rim of the platter and serve.

## cook's tip

Tabbouleh is a classic Middle
Eastern grain salad made with
bulgur wheat, tomatoes, and
parsley. Hummus is a spread
made from puréed chickpeas
(garbanzo beans) and tahini,
or sesame seed paste. Both are
available in the cold case of
many well-stocked supermarkets
and delicatessens.

# asian chicken salad

### 1 Make the dressing

In a blender, combine the chopped onion, ginger, miso, vinegar, honey, canola oil, and sesame oil. Pulse until smooth.

### 2 Assemble the salad

In a large bowl, combine the onion slices, bell pepper, bean sprouts, chicken, and cilantro. Add the dressing and toss to coat evenly. Arrange on a plate and serve.

**Red onion,** ½ small, thinly sliced, plus 2 tablespoons finely chopped

**Ginger,** 1 teaspoon finely grated

**White miso,** 1½ tablespoons

**Rice vinegar,** 3 tablespoons

**Honey,** 1 tablespoon

**Canola oil,** 5 tablespoons (2½ fl oz/75 ml)

**Asian sesame oil,** 2 tablespoons

**Red or yellow bell pepper (capsicum),** 1, seeded and thinly sliced

**Bean sprouts,** ⅔ cup (2 oz/ 60 g)

**Cooked chicken breasts, poached (page 26) or rotisserie,** 4 cups, (1½ lbs (750 g), shredded

**Fresh cilantro (fresh coriander),** ¼ cup (⅓ oz/ 10 g) coarsely chopped

SERVES 4

85

# mushroom, radicchio & bulgur salad

**Cremini mushrooms,** 2 lb (1 kg), halved

**Olive oil,** ⅓ cup (3 fl oz/ 80 ml), plus 2 tablespoons

**Garlic,** 3 cloves, coarsely chopped

**Salt and freshly ground pepper**

**Thick-cut pancetta or bacon,** 3 oz (90 g), chopped

**Whole-grain bulgur,** 1 cup (6 oz/185 g)

**Radicchio,** 1 head, cored and thinly sliced

**Sherry vinegar,** 1 tablespoon

**Parmesan cheese,** 2 oz (60 g), shaved

SERVES 4

### 1 Cook the mushrooms and pancetta

Preheat the oven to 475°F (245°C). In a large roasting pan, combine the mushrooms, ⅓ cup oil, and garlic. Season generously with salt and pepper and toss to coat evenly. Spread the mushrooms in a single layer. Roast for 5 minutes, turn the mushrooms, and continue roasting until the edges are crisp, 2–3 minutes longer. In a frying pan over medium heat, cook the pancetta, stirring occasionally, until crisp, about 10 minutes. Using a slotted spoon, transfer to paper towels to drain.

### 2 Cook the bulgur

In a frying pan over medium-high heat, toast the bulgur until its nutty aroma is released, 3–4 minutes. Add 2 cups (16 fl oz/500 ml) boiling water and 1 teaspoon salt to the bulgur, cover, and simmer over low heat until tender, about 20 minutes; or, cook according to the package directions. Transfer to a large stainless-steel bowl. Add the radicchio and the 2 tablespoons oil and toss to combine.

### 3 Assemble the salad

Add the roasted mushrooms, pancetta, vinegar, ½ teaspoon salt, and a pinch of pepper to the radicchio. Toss to combine and spoon onto individual plates. Top with the Parmesan and serve.

## cook's tip

A mixture of wild or cultivated mushrooms, such as chanterelle, shiitake, morel, or porcini, can be substituted for the cremini mushrooms. If you have a hard time finding different varieties, you can use button mushrooms or portobello mushrooms. If using portobello, cut into 1-inch (2.5-cm) cubes before roasting.

water for about 20 minutes,
then drained and chopped.
Oil-packed tomatoes need
only be removed from the
oil and chopped. Use 1 cup
(3 oz/90 g) dry-packed
tomatoes or 1 cup (5 oz/
155 g) drained oil-packed
tomatoes.

# chicken & roasted tomato salad

## 1 Roast the tomatoes

Preheat the oven to 350°F (180°C). Oil a large rimmed baking sheet. Arrange the tomatoes, cut side up, on the prepared sheet in a single layer. Brush with 2 tablespoons of the olive oil, sprinkle with thyme, and season with salt and pepper. Roast the tomatoes until shriveled on top but still juicy underneath, about 50 minutes. Let cool on the baking sheet. (The tomatoes can be made ahead of time, covered with plastic wrap, and set aside for up to 4 hours at room temperature or overnight in the refrigerator.) Cut the tomatoes in half again before using.

## 2 Cook the chicken

Season both sides of each chicken breast with salt and pepper. In a large frying pan over medium heat, melt the butter with the canola oil. Add the chicken and cook, turning once, until golden brown and firm, 4–5 minutes per side. Transfer to a cutting board and let stand for 5 minutes.

## 3 Assemble the salad

Place the arugula in a large bowl, drizzle with the remaining 4 tablespoons (2 fl oz/60 ml) olive oil, and toss to coat evenly. Sprinkle with the vinegar, ¼ teaspoon salt, and a pinch of pepper, and toss again. Arrange the arugula on plates. Cut the chicken on the diagonal into slices and place on the arugula. Garnish with the roasted tomatoes, top with the Parmesan, and serve.

**Plum (Roma) tomatoes,**
1½ lb (750 g), halved
lengthwise and seeded

**Fresh thyme leaves,**
1 tablespoon

**Olive oil,** 6 tablespoons
(3 fl oz/90 ml)

**Salt and freshly ground
pepper**

**Skinless, boneless chicken
breasts,** 1¼ lb (625 g),
pounded lightly to an even
thickness

**Unsalted butter,**
2 tablespoons

**Canola oil,** 1 tablespoon

**Arugula (rocket),** 6 oz
(185 g)

**Balsamic vinegar,**
1½ tablespoons

**Parmesan cheese,** 2 oz
(60 g), shaved

SERVES 4

# chipotle beef
## & corn salad

**Boneless sirloin or rib-eye steak,** 1 ¼ lb (625 g) and 1 ½ inches (4 cm) thick

**Olive oil,** ¼ cup (2 fl oz/ 60 ml), plus 2 tablespoons

**Salt and freshly ground pepper**

**Canned chipotle chiles in adobo,** ¼ cup (1 ½ oz/45 g) with sauce

**Lime juice,** from 2 limes

**White wine vinegar,** 1 tablespoon

**Garlic,** 1 large clove, sliced

**Corn kernels,** from 2 ears of corn (about 2 cups/12 oz/ 375 g)

**Radishes,** 6, chopped

**Plum (Roma) tomatoes,** 4, chopped

**Fresh cilantro (fresh coriander),** ¼ cup (⅓ oz/ 10 g) minced

**Romaine (cos) lettuce,** 2 heads, pale inner leaves only, torn into bite-sized pieces

SERVES 4

1 Marinate the steak
Place the steak on a plate, brush both sides with the 2 tablespoons oil, and season both sides generously with salt and pepper. Let stand for 30 minutes.

2 Make the dressing and corn salsa
Meanwhile, in a blender, combine the chipotle chiles, the ¼ cup oil, half of the lime juice, the vinegar, garlic, 1 tablespoon water, ¼ teaspoon salt, and a pinch of pepper. Process until smooth. In a bowl, toss together the corn, radishes, tomatoes, cilantro, the remaining lime juice, and ¼ teaspoon salt.

3 Cook the steak and assemble the salad
Prepare a gas or charcoal grill for direct grilling over medium-high heat. Alternatively, preheat a stovetop grill pan over medium-high heat. Place the steak on the grill rack or in the grill pan and cook, turning every 4 minutes, about 8 minutes total per side for medium-rare. Transfer to a cutting board and let stand for 5–10 minutes. Cut the steak on the diagonal across the grain into thin slices. Arrange the lettuce on plates and top with the beef and corn salsa. Drizzle with the dressing and serve.

## cook's tip

Chipotle chiles, fresh jalapeños that have been dried and then smoked, are preserved in a spicy, vinegary tomato sauce called adobo. Cans of chipotle chiles in adobo are now available in most supermarkets. Transfer unused chiles and sauce to a glass jar with a tight cap and refrigerate for up to 6 months.

## cook's tip

If you can't find Israeli couscous, substitute 1½ cups (9 oz/280 g) instant couscous: place in a heatproof bowl; bring 2¾ cups (22 fl oz/680 ml) broth to a boil with the onion, salt, and pepper; pour over the couscous; stir; and let stand for 15 minutes. Or, boil 10 oz (315 g) orzo pasta until al dente, drain, and toss with the cooked onion, salt, pepper, oil, mint, and lemon juice.

# grilled lamb & couscous salad

**1 Season the lamb**

Place the lamb in a large baking dish and brush both sides with the 2 tablespoons olive oil. Season generously with salt and pepper and the thyme. Let stand for up to 1 hour at room temperature or up to 2 hours in the refrigerator (return to room temperature before cooking).

**2 Cook the couscous**

In a saucepan over medium heat, warm the canola oil. Add the onion and cook, stirring occasionally, until softened, about 5 minutes. Add the couscous and cook, stirring, until just beginning to brown, about 6 minutes. Add the broth, 1 teaspoon salt, and a pinch of pepper. Bring to a boil, reduce the heat to low, cover, and simmer until the couscous is tender and all the liquid is absorbed, about 8 minutes. Remove from the heat and stir in the ¼ cup oil and the mint.

**3 Cook the lamb and assemble the salad**

Prepare a gas or charcoal grill for direct grilling over high heat. Alternatively, preheat a grill pan over high heat. Place the lamb slices on the grill rack or in the grill pan and cook, turning once, until rare or medium-rare, 2–3 minutes per side. Transfer to a cutting board and let rest for 5 minutes. Cut into thin strips. Add the lemon juice to the couscous. Taste and adjust the seasoning with salt, pepper, and lemon juice, then fluff again. Spoon the couscous on plates and surround with the salad greens. Top with the lamb and serve.

**Boneless leg of lamb,** 1¼ lb (625 g), cut into thick slices

**Olive oil,** ¼ cup (2 fl oz/ 60 ml), plus 2 tablespoons

**Salt and freshly ground pepper**

**Dried thyme,** ¼ teaspoon

**Canola oil,** 1 tablespoon

**Yellow onion,** 1 small, finely chopped

**Israeli couscous,** 1½ cups (6 oz/185 g)

**Chicken broth,** 2 cups (16 fl oz/500 ml)

**Fresh mint,** ¼ cup (⅓ oz/ 10 g) minced

**Lemon juice,** from 1 lemon

**Mixed baby greens,** 2 oz (60 g)

SERVES 4

# the smarter cook

A main-dish salad can turn simple elements—fresh greens and vegetables, shredded chicken or sliced steak, and a tangy vinaigrette—into a nourishing meal. Salads can be healthful and infinitely varied. Best of all, they don't require many steps or complicated cooking techniques. All you need are simple, yet creative recipes like the ones in this book, a well-stocked pantry, and a weekly meal plan.

In these pages, you'll find strategies and ideas for managing your kitchen and making salads a regular part of your weeknight meals. With a little organization and some advance prep on the weekend, you can spend less time shopping and cooking and more time enjoying delicious food during the week. It all adds up to smarter cooking—making life easier without sacrificing quality.

# get started

When it comes to salads, the secret of smarter cooking is planning ahead. This means working out a meal plan for the week; thinking about how prep, shopping, and cooking can fit into your schedule; and stocking up on pantry, refrigerated, and frozen items (pages 104 to 107). Once you do, you will be able to create great salads in record time any night of the week.

## plan a meal around salad

During the weekend, make a meal plan for the week. This will save you hours of shopping and prep time and alleviate the last-minute stress of deciding what to feed your family each night. Once you have worked out your menus, make a list of the vegetables, meat, poultry, and seafood you will need to supplement what's in your pantry.

- **A salad can be a complete meal.** With just a few accompaniments (see Round It Out, page 97), most of the salads in this book can be served as complete meals. Adding main-dish salads to your weeknight menus is both healthful and time-saving, as they are generally rich in vegetables and require little cooking.

- **Salad can also be a first course.** When you have extra time or are entertaining guests, you can prepare any of these salads as a starter simply by reducing the portion size by up to one-half.

- **Salads should reflect the season.** Choose recipes that make the most of the freshest ingredients of the season. You'll enjoy the best flavor and save money, because in-season ingredients are often less expensive. Visit a local farmers' market for inspiration and the freshest fruits and vegetables (see Think Seasonally, right).

- **Mix and match components.** Once you find salad recipes you like, you can use their basic elements (dressing, greens, protein, vegetables, croutons, and toppings) to create new combinations of your own. When preparing a salad, make extra dressing or other components to use in another salad later in the week.

**THINK SEASONALLY**

**spring** Serve simple salads with light citrus dressings that showcase the delicate flavors of spring: asparagus, artichokes, beets, fava (broad) beans, fresh herbs (such as dill, chives, and mint), green (spring) onions, leeks, new potatoes, and peas.

**summer** Prepare refreshing salads with abundant summer vegetables and fruits: bell peppers (capsicums), berries, corn, cucumbers, eggplants (aubergines), fresh basil, peaches and other stone fruits, tomatoes, and zucchini (courgette) and other summer squashes.

**autumn** Accent green salads and cabbage slaws with apples, figs, pears, and persimmons. Toss steamed or roasted seasonal produce, including winter squashes, broccoli, cauliflower, mushrooms, and sweet potatoes, in full-flavored dressings.

**winter** Build salads around hearty winter greens, such as Belgian endive (chicory/witloof), cabbage, escarole (Batavian endive), and watercress. Pair with seasonal vegetables and fruits, such as celery root (celeriac), citrus, fennel, mushrooms, and winter squashes.

## ROUND IT OUT

**bread** Serve warm crusty bread, baguettes, or focaccia with extra-virgin olive oil. Or, buy corn bread, warm it briefly in the oven just before dinner, and serve it with softened butter. Accompany Mediterranean salads with warm pita wedges or with bruschetta (toasted country bread slices rubbed with a halved garlic clove and sprinkled with extra-virgin olive oil, salt, and pepper). Accompany Latin-inspired salads with fresh tortillas, warmed by wrapping them in a clean kitchen towel and microwaving them for 30 seconds.

**sliced meats** Assemble an assortment of sliced prosciutto, salami, smoked turkey, and other deli meats. Serve on a platter or cutting board with bread or breadsticks on the side.

**cheeses** Just before you begin preparing dinner, set out two or three good-quality cheeses—including a soft, creamy one and a harder slicing one—so they can come to room temperature. Serve with baguette rounds or crackers.

**vegetables** Serve warm or room-temperature steamed, sautéed, or roasted vegetables seasoned with salt, pepper, and a little butter or olive oil. For extra flavor, add lemon juice, fresh herbs, or grated Parmesan cheese.

**soup** Hot or cold, homemade or store-bought, soup pairs perfectly with a simple salad. Keep servings of your favorite soup recipes on hand in the freezer so you can have a ready-made soup-and-salad meal anytime.

# sample meals

IN MINUTES meals can be made when time is especially short. FIT FOR COMPANY meals are easy ideas for stress-free get-togethers when you want to make an impression.

| IN MINUTES | FIT FOR COMPANY |
|---|---|
| **Chicken & Orzo Salad** (page 10) Garlic and herb crostini Assorted cheeses | **Flank Steak, Arugula & Potato Salad** (page 81) Grilled corn with herb butter *Syrah or Merlot* |
| **Spinach, Pear & Walnut Salad** (page 13) Rotisserie chicken | **Antipasto Salad** (page 33) Ravioli with butter and sage *Full-bodied Italian white wine* |
| **Grapefruit, Jicama & Avocado Salad** (page 17) Warm corn tortillas | **Crab Cake & Butter Lettuce Salad** (page 73) Toasted focaccia wedges *Sauvignon Blanc* |
| **Tuna & White Bean Salad** (page 21) Sliced heirloom tomatoes Crusty bread | **Grilled Summer Vegetable Salad** (page 55) Grilled halibut with pesto *Pinot Noir or dry Rosé* |
| **Greek Salad with Herbed Pita** (page 25) Hummus or baba ghanoush | **Mediterranean Meze** (page 82) Pan-seared lamb chops with herbs Oven-roasted potato wedges *Syrah or Zinfandel* |
| **Thai Steak & Bok Choy Salad** (page 18) Steamed rice noodles with basil | |

# make it easy

Salads can be easily adapted to suit any taste—and to make use of whatever you have on hand in your refrigerator or pantry. Use the recipes in this book as a starting point, building on them with these simple ideas and tips to create your own quick and satisfying salads.

- **Wash greens well.** Fill a large bowl with cold water. Trim off the stem end of each head of lettuce and pull the leaves apart. Cut or tear into bite-sized pieces and toss into the water. Allow the greens to float to the top and let them stand for a few minutes. Dry in a salad spinner in small batches. (For storage tips, see page 106.)

- **Refresh greens.** To revive lettuce that is beginning to wilt, soak it in a bowl of ice water in the refrigerator for 30 minutes to 1 hour. When ready to use the lettuce, drain and dry as directed above.

- **Create contrasts.** Try to achieve a mix of colors, textures, flavors, sizes, and shapes when combining salad ingredients. For example, if you add a soft ingredient, such as avocado or blue cheese, balance it with something crunchy, like jicama or toasted walnuts. Add brightly colored ingredients, such as radishes, oranges, or beets, to offset paler greens. Complement sweet and rich flavors with bright, acidic ingredients.

- **Think beyond lettuce.** You can toss virtually any vegetable with dressing to make a salad. Add coarsely chopped fresh herbs such as dill, basil, chives, mint, and flat-leaf (Italian) parsley to salads for additional flavor and color.

- **Taste before you toss.** To taste a salad dressing, try it on a single leaf of lettuce, rather than tasting it with a spoon. You will get a better sense of how it will taste in the finished salad. Adjust the seasonings, adding more oil or acidic ingredients if needed, before dressing the salad.

- **Add dressing sparingly.** For lettuce salads, add the dressing just before serving to keep the greens from wilting. Err on the side of underdressing, using just enough dressing to moisten the greens. You can pass extra at the table for those who want to add more.

---

## SIMPLE SALADS

**butter lettuce salad** Combine Dijon mustard, white wine vinegar, and extra-virgin olive oil in the bottom of a salad bowl. Add torn butter (Boston) lettuce leaves and snipped chives and toss.

**insalata caprese** For this classic summer salad, alternate slices of ripe tomato and fresh mozzarella on a platter. Sprinkle with fresh basil leaves, drizzle with extra-virgin olive oil, and season with salt and pepper.

**mediterranean summer salad** Toss chunks of peeled cucumber and ripe tomato (or halved cherry tomatoes) with sliced green (spring) or red onion, Kalamata olives, fresh oregano or mint, and crumbled feta cheese in a red wine vinaigrette.

**warm spinach salad** Fry a few strips of bacon, then drain and chop. Make a dressing with cider vinegar, minced shallots, olive oil, and a little of the bacon drippings. Warm the dressing and toss with the spinach. Top with chopped hard-boiled egg and the bacon.

**chopped salad** Wash and dry iceberg lettuce and hearts of romaine (cos) lettuce. Toss with diced apples or pears, toasted pecans or walnuts, dried cranberries or raisins, crumbled goat cheese, and chunks of smoked turkey or chicken in a honey-mustard dressing.

**fennel-orange salad** Trim and thinly slice two fennel bulbs. Peel regular or blood oranges and slice crosswise. Gently toss with minced shallot and a champagne vinaigrette.

**mustard vinaigrette** In a bowl, whisk together 2 cloves minced garlic, 1 minced shallot, 3 tablespoons red wine vinegar, and 1 tablespoon Dijon mustard. Gradually add ½ cup (4 fl oz/ 125 ml) olive oil, whisking constantly to form an emulsion. Season to taste with salt and pepper.

**blue cheese dressing** In a bowl, whisk together 2 tablespoons white wine vinegar, 1 teaspoon Worcestershire sauce, 2 teaspoons Dijon mustard, ¼ cup (2 fl oz/60 ml) mayonnaise, and ¼ cup (2 fl oz/60 ml) olive oil. Gently stir in ¼ cup (1 oz/30 g) crumbled blue cheese just until combined. Season to taste with salt and pepper.

**caesar dressing** In a food processor, combine 1 teaspoon red wine vinegar, 2 tablespoons fresh lemon juice, 1 teaspoon Worcestershire sauce, 1 tablespoon mayonnaise, ½ teaspoon salt, a generous amount of freshly ground pepper, 2 cloves minced garlic, 1–3 finely chopped anchovies (optional), 2 teaspoons Dijon mustard, and ¼ cup (2 fl oz/60 ml) canola or olive oil. Pulse until completely smooth.

**asian sesame-miso dressing** In a food processor, combine 1 clove chopped garlic, 2 tablespoons chopped red onion, 1 teaspoon grated fresh ginger, 1½ tablespoons white miso, 3 tablespoons rice vinegar, 1 tablespoon honey, 5 tablespoons (2½ fl oz/75 ml) canola oil, 2 tablespoons Asian sesame oil, and a pinch of cayenne pepper. Pulse until smooth.

# vinaigrette basics

The classic formula for vinaigrette dressing is 1 part vinegar to 3 parts oil, plus salt and pepper to taste. Use these proportions as a guideline.

▪ For the easiest vinaigrette, simply drizzle olive oil and good-quality vinegar over your salad, followed by plenty of coarse salt and freshly ground pepper and toss.

▪ To create smooth, emulsified dressings, combine all the ingredients except the oil in a bowl. Add the oil in a slow, steady stream as you whisk constantly with a small whisk or fork. Or, use a blender or mini food processor to eliminate the guesswork.

▪ Make extra dressing and store it in a jar or airtight container in the refrigerator to use later in the week.

▪ When making vinaigrettes, experiment with different kinds of vinegar, such as balsamic, cider, rice, or a flavor-infused vinegar. Or, substitute fresh citrus juice, such as lemon or lime, for half of the vinegar.

▪ Try using different types of oil in your dressings: a small amount of walnut or hazelnut (filbert) oil adds rich, nutty of flavor to an otherwise standard vinaigrette.

▪ Make your own flavored oils by infusing extra-virgin olive oil with minced herbs, citrus zest, chile, or other flavorings. Use the same day, or store in a stopped glass bottle in the refrigerator for a few weeks. Check for freshness before using.

▪ For extra flavor, add minced shallots to a vinaigrette, allowing them to sit in the dressing for 30 minutes or more.

▪ Whisk mustard, yogurt, mayonnaise, or sour cream into vinaigrettes for a creamier flavor and consistency.

▪ Liven up the flavor of store-bought dressings by adding fresh ingredients, such as herbs, lemon juice, garlic, shallots, or yogurt.

▪ Use vinaigrettes to marinate foods for grilling or to drizzle over warm vegetables just before serving.

# use shortcut ingredients

Smart cooks rely on high-quality prepared foods to help get dinner on the table in a hurry. These ingredients make the job easier, either because they are already assembled and ready to use or because they add concentrated flavor without extra work. Here are some salad-making time-savers.

**bottled dressings** Keep a variety of dressings on hand to use when you're pressed for time. Look for dressings and vinaigrettes that include all-natural ingredients.

**canned beans** Keep cannellini beans, chickpeas (garbanzo beans), and other legumes in your pantry. Before adding to salads, drain and rinse under cold water. Or, heat briefly with sautéed onion, garlic, or herbs for extra flavor, then let cool before using.

**cherry tomatoes** Purchase red and gold cherry tomatoes, rinse them, drain and dry them well, and return them to their containers. Store at room temperature; toss whole or halved into salads.

**croutons** Store-bought or homemade croutons add texture to all kinds of salads and will keep for a few weeks in an airtight container in the pantry. To make croutons, remove crusts from country bread or a baguette and cut into cubes. Fry the cubes in olive oil, with or without seasonings, until golden.

**crumbled cheese** Buy crumbled goat, feta, or blue cheese, and keep in the refrigerator to toss into salads.

**frozen cleaned shrimp** Keep a bag of peeled, deveined cooked shrimp (prawns) or bay shrimp in the freezer. They can be quickly thawed under running cold water and used to turn almost any salad into a more substantial meal.

**mozzarella cheese** Look for bite-sized fresh mozzarella balls, which can be tossed directly into salads without any prep.

**nuts** Buy spiced or candied walnuts, pecans, almonds, or other nuts to sprinkle on salads.

**olives** Keep a variety of pitted olives on hand for adding to salads, either whole or coarsely chopped.

**parmesan cheese** Keep a wedge of good-quality Parmesan cheese on hand to shave over salads with a vegetable peeler.

**prewashed salad greens** Buy cut-up mixed lettuces, spinach, romaine (cos), iceberg, slaw mix, and other salad greens in bags or plastic boxes.

**rotisserie chicken** Buy an extra rotisserie chicken, which can be quickly boned, skinned, and chopped for tossing into salads during the week.

**salad bar vegetables** At the supermarket salad bar, fill a container with prepped and/or cooked vegetables, such as beets, broccoli, potatoes, snap peas, snow peas (mangetouts), cauliflower, and carrots to use in salads.

**sauces and condiments** Stock up on a broad variety of prepared sauces and bottled ingredients, such as tapenade, pesto, Asian peanut sauce, capers, roasted red peppers (capsicums), marinated vegetables, and chutneys. Store them in the pantry and refrigerator to have on hand for perking up salads.

**soy sauce** Add a few drops of soy sauce to salad dressings to enhance and round out flavors.

**tuna in oil** Look for imported tuna packed in olive oil in jars or cans for a quick protein addition.

# shop smarter

Good-quality fresh ingredients make cooking easier because they deliver the best flavor with the least effort. Get to know a reliable produce vendor, butcher, fishmonger, and specialty-food shop merchant in your area so you can ask for recommendations on what's in season. Call ahead to place your order so it is ready to pick up on your way home from work.

## MAKE A SHOPPING LIST

**prepare in advance** Make a list of what you need to buy before you go shopping and you'll save time at the store.

**make a template** Create a list template on your computer, then fill it in during the week before you go shopping.

**categorize your lists** Use the following categories to keep your lists organized: pantry, fresh, and occasional.

■ **pantry items** Check the pantry and write down any items that need to be restocked to make the meals on your weekly plan.

■ **fresh ingredients** These are for immediate use and include produce, seafood, meats, and some cheeses. You might need to visit different stores or supermarket sections, so divide the list into subcategories, such as produce, dairy, and meats.

■ **occasional items** This is a revolving list for refrigerated items that are replaced as needed, such as butter and eggs.

**be flexible** Be ready to change your menus based on the freshest ingredients at the market.

■ **Salad greens** When buying lettuce, spinach, and other greens and herbs, look for bright color and light, fresh texture. Avoid greens that appear wilted, discolored, compacted, or soggy. When purchasing prewashed packaged greens, choose those with the freshest appearance and the latest expiration date. Make a point of trying new greens, asking your produce vendor for serving recommendations.

■ **Produce** If there is a farmers' market in your area, get into the habit of visiting it often. It's an excellent way to keep tabs on what is in season, and you will often find good deals on bumper-crop produce. Choose vegetables and fruits that are free of bruises and blemishes and feel heavy for their size. Vegetables such as eggplants (aubergines) and zucchini (courgettes) should have taut skins, bright color, and be firm to the touch. Mushrooms should be firm and plump looking and neither wet and soggy nor dry and wrinkled.

■ **Meat and poultry** Look for meat with good, uniform color and a fresh smell. Any fat should be bright white, not waxy looking. If your recipes call for boned meat, ask the butcher to bone it for you and to trim external fat. This will save you time, and removing the fat will help prevent flare-ups if you will be grilling. Poultry should be plump, with smooth skin and firm flesh, and any visible flesh should be white to light yellow.

■ **Seafood** Always ask the fishmonger which fish and shellfish are freshest, and then examine them carefully before you buy. You want to look for bright color, a moist and shiny surface, clear eyes, and little or no "fishy" smell. Buying cleaned squid and deveined shrimp (prawns) will save you prep time.

# the well-stocked kitchen

Stay on top of the ingredients in your kitchen, and you will always be able to turn out a quick main-dish salad, even on short notice. A well-stocked and well-ordered kitchen will save you time searching, prepping, and running to the store for last-minute items when you're ready to make dinner. You'll also find that you will shop less frequently and spend less time at the store when you do.

Here's a guide to the essential ingredients you need to make the recipes in this book, along with tips for keeping everything properly stored and organized. Use it to help take stock of what's in your kitchen. Then plan a shopping trip, and set aside some time to get your pantry in order. It is an investment in smarter cooking that will make your life a little easier, whether you're making a salad or a multicourse meal.

# the pantry

A pantry is typically a closet or one or more cupboards in which you store dried, canned, and jarred foods, such as herbs, and spices, beans, grains, and pasta, as well as garlic, onions, potatoes, and other fresh items that don't need refrigeration. The pantry should be relatively cool, dry, and dark. Avoid cupboards immediately adjacent to the stove, which can be too warm for storing food.

## stock your pantry

- Take inventory of your pantry using the Pantry Staples list.

- Remove everything from the pantry, clean the shelves and line with paper, if needed, then resort items by type.

- Discard items that have passed their expiration date or have a stale or otherwise questionable appearance or odor.

- Make a list of items that you need to replace or stock.

- Shop for the items on your list.

- Restock the pantry, organizing it so everything is easy to find.

- Write the purchase date on perishable items and clearly label bulk items. Keep a marking pen and tape in the pantry for this purpose.

- Arrange staples you use often in the most accessible part of the pantry.

- Store dried herbs and spices in well-sealed containers, preferably in a separate spice or herb organizer, shelf, or drawer.

## keep it organized

- Look over the recipes in your weekly meal plan and check your pantry to make sure you have all the ingredients you'll need.

- Rotate items as you use them, moving the oldest ones to the front of the pantry so they will be used first.

- Keep a list of the items you use up so you can replace them.

---

### STORING VINEGAR

Vinegars should be stored in well-sealed containers in a cool, dark place. Exposure to light can affect both the appearance and the flavor. Unopened bottles will keep almost indefinitely. Once opened, most vinegars will keep, at room temperature, for up to 1 year. Smell or taste vinegar that has been exposed to light and air for signs of spoilage.

---

### STORING OIL

All oils are sensitive to heat and light. Unopened bottles of oil can be stored at room temperature in a cool, dark place for a few months, but their flavor will diminish over time. Store opened bottles of olive oil and other vegetable oils at room temperature for up to 3 months or in the refrigerator for up to 6 months. Most specialty oils, such as Asian sesame oil, walnut oil, or oils flavored with garlic, herbs, or other seasonings, should be stored in the refrigerator once they have been opened, as they can spoil or turn rancid quickly.

## PANTRY STORAGE

**dried herbs & spices** Dried herbs and spices start losing flavor after 6 months. Buy them in small quantities, store in airtight containers labeled with purchase date, and replace often.

**fresh foods** Some fresh foods, such as potatoes, onions, shallots, and garlic, are best kept at room temperature. Store in a cool, dark place and check occasionally for sprouting and spoilage. Don't store potatoes alongside onions; when placed next to each other, they produce gases that hasten spoilage.

**fruits & vegetables** Some fruits and vegetables, such as pears, tomatoes, and many summer fruits, retain their flavor and texture better when stored at room temperature. Store fruits uncovered on a countertop. To speed the ripening of apples, peaches, and other fruits, put in a paper bag with a banana. The banana naturally emits ethylene gas, which will ripen its companions.

**canned foods** Discard canned foods if the cans show signs of expansion or buckling. Once a can is opened, transfer the unused contents to an airtight container and refrigerate for later use.

**grains & pasta** Store grains in airtight containers for up to 3 months. The shelf life of most dried pastas is up to 1 year. Although it is technically safe to eat beyond that time, they will have lost some flavor. Once you open a package, store what you don't use in an airtight container.

## PANTRY STAPLES

### DRIED HERBS & SPICES

black pepper

cayenne pepper

coriander

cumin

oregano

paprika

red pepper flakes

salt

thyme

### OILS

Asian sesame oil

canola oil

corn oil

extra-virgin olive oil

### VINEGARS

balsamic vinegar

champagne vinegar

red wine vinegar

rice vinegar

sherry vinegar

white wine vinegar

### SAUCES & CONDIMENTS

Asian fish sauce

hot-pepper sauce

mayonnaise

miso, white or red

mustards: Dijon, honey Dijon, spicy tarragon, whole-grain

soy sauce

Worcestershire sauce

### CANNED & JARRED FOODS

black beans

capers

chicken broth

chickpeas (garbanzo beans)

roasted red bell peppers (capsicums)

tomatoes, canned

tuna packed in olive oil

white beans

### GRAINS, LEGUMES & PASTAS

couscous, instant

flour, all-purpose (plain)

fusilli

lentils, French green

orzo

rice vermicelli

### WINE & SPIRITS

red wine

vermouth, dry

white wine

### MISCELLANEOUS

almonds, slivered

bread crumbs, dried

corn tortillas

currants

honey

*panko*

pecans

pine nuts

pita bread

# the refrigerator

Once you've stocked and organized your pantry, you can apply the same time-saving strategies to your refrigerator. The refrigerator is ideal for storing meats, poultry, seafood, greens and other vegetables, and leftovers. Check the produce bins of your refrigerator regularly for forgotten foods that have gone bad. Salad greens and fresh herbs are particularly susceptible to spoilage.

## general tips

- Foods lose flavor if not refrigerated correctly, so proper storage and an even temperature of below 40°F (5°C) is important.

- Don't crowd foods in the refrigerator or freezer. Air should circulate freely to keep foods evenly cooled.

- Check the contents of the refrigerator at least once a week and discard any old or spoiled food.

## salad storage

- Store washed greens (page 98) loosely wrapped in a clean kitchen towel or paper towels in a resealable plastic bag. Gently press the air out of the bag before sealing. Use bags that each hold enough greens for a single meal. Stored in this way in the crisper of your refrigerator, most greens will keep for up to 1 week.

- Store leftover salad dressings in well-sealed, nonreactive containers in the refrigerator.

## cheese storage

- Wrap cheeses well to prevent them from drying out. Hard cheeses, such as Parmesan, keep longer than fresh cheeses, such as some goat cheeses. Use fresh cheeses within a few days. Store soft and semisoft cheeses for up to 2 weeks, and hard cheeses for up to 1 month.

### KEEP IT ORGANIZED

**clean first** Remove items a few at a time and wash the refrigerator with warm, soapy water, then rinse well with clean water. Wash and rinse your freezer at the same time.

**rotate items** Discard any items that have exceeded their expiration dates, and throw away any items that have a questionable smell or appearance.

**stock up** Use the list on the opposite page as a starting point to decide which items you need to buy or replace.

**shop** Shop for the items on your list.

**date of purchase** Label items you plan to keep for more than a few weeks, writing the date directly on the package or on a piece of masking tape.

### STORING WINE

Once wine is uncorked, exposure to air causes it to oxidize and become sour. Store opened wine in the refrigerator for up to 3 days. Use a vacuum wine pump to prolong shelf life.

# fresh herb & vegetable storage

▓ Wrap fresh herbs in a damp paper towel, slip into a plastic bag, and store in the crisper. Rinse and stem herbs just before using.

▓ To store parsley, trim the stem ends, stand the bunch in a glass of water, drape a plastic bag loosely over the leaves, and refrigerate.

▓ If you find you have extra fresh herbs, freeze them for later use. Rinse them, pat them dry, remove the stems, and freeze the leaves on a baking sheet. Once the leaves are frozen, transfer to resealable plastic bags. Herbs can also be puréed in a food processor to make a paste, which can be frozen in ice-cube trays or resealable plastic bags.

▓ Sturdy vegetables will keep for up to 1 week in the refrigerator, while more delicate ones will keep for only a few days.

▓ Cut about ½ inch (12 mm) off the end of each asparagus spear, stand the spears, tips up, in a glass of cold water, and refrigerate, changing the water daily. Stored in this way, asparagus will keep for up to 1 week.

▓ Store tomatoes, eggplants (aubergines), and winter squashes, such as butternut, at room temperature.

# meat, poultry & seafood storage

▓ Most seafood should be used the same day you purchase it.

▓ Use or freeze fresh meat and poultry within 2 days of purchase. If buying packaged meats or poultry, check the expiration date and use before that date.

▓ Place packaged meats on a plate in the coldest part of the refrigerator. If only a portion of the meat is used, discard the original packaging and rewrap in fresh wrapping.

▓ When freezing raw meat, poultry, or seafood, remove it from the original packaging and wrap in one- or two-serving portions, which can be individually thawed as needed.

# index

### OXMOOR HOUSE

Oxmoor House books are distributed by Sunset Books
80 Willow Road, Menlo Park, CA 94025
Telephone: 650 321 3600  Fax: 650 324 1532

**Vice President/General Manager**  Rich Smeby
**National Accounts Manager/Special Sales**  Brad Moses
Oxmoor House and Sunset Books are divisions of
Southern Progress Corporation

### WILLIAMS-SONOMA

**Founder & Vice-Chairman**  Chuck Williams

### THE WILLIAMS-SONOMA FOOD MADE FAST SERIES

Conceived and produced by Weldon Owen Inc.
814 Montgomery Street, San Francisco, CA 94133
Telephone: 415 291 0100  Fax: 415 291 8841

In collaboration with Williams-Sonoma, Inc.
3250 Van Ness Avenue, San Francisco, CA 94109

**Photographers**  Tucker + Hossler
**Food Stylist**  Jennifer Straus
**Food Stylist's Assistant**  Max La Rivière-Hedrick
**Text Writer**  Steve Siegelman

Library of Congress Cataloging-in-Publication data is available.
ISBN-13: 978-0-8487-3146-5
ISBN-10: 0-8487-3146-8

### WELDON OWEN INC.

**Chief Executive Officer**  John Owen
**President and Chief Operating Officer**  Terry Newell
**Chief Financial Officer**  Christine E. Munson
**Vice President International Sales**  Stuart Laurence
**Vice President and Creative Director**  Gaye Allen
**Vice President and Publisher**  Hannah Rahill
**Art Director**  Kyrie Forbes Panton
**Senior Editor**  Kim Goodfriend
**Editor**  Emily Miller
**Designer and Photo Director**  Andrea Stephany
**Associate Editor**  Lauren Hancock
**Assistant Editor**  Juli Vendzules
**Production Director**  Chris Hemesath
**Color Manager**  Teri Bell
**Production and Reprint Coordinator**  Todd Rechner

### A WELDON OWEN PRODUCTION

Set in Formata
First printed in 2006
10 9 8 7 6 5 4 3 2 1
Color separations by Bright Arts Singapore
Printed by Tien Wah Press

Printed in Singapore

### ACKNOWLEDGMENTS
Weldon Owen wishes to thank the following people for their generous support in producing this book:
Heather Belt, Kevin Crafts, Ken DellaPenta, Judith Dunham, Alexa Hyman, Marianne Mitten, Sharon Silva, and Kate Washington.

Cover photograph by Bill Bettencourt: Grilled Chicken Caesar, page 48.
Cover photograph styled by Kevin Crafts.

### A NOTE ON WEIGHTS AND MEASURES
All recipes include customary U.S. and metric measurements. Metric conversions are based on
a standard developed for these books and have been rounded off. Actual weights may vary.